MAGNA CARTA AND
THE IDEA OF LIBERTY

MAJOR ISSUES IN HISTORY

Editor

C. WARREN HOLLISTER

University of California, Santa Barbara

MAGNA CARTA AND THE IDEA OF LIBERTY

EDITED BY

James C. Holt

John Wiley & Sons, Inc.,
New York • London • Sydney • Toronto

Library of Congress Catalogue Card Number: 70-38963

ISBN 0-471-40845-X (cloth)
ISBN 0-471-40843-3 (paper)

Printed in the United States of America.

10 9 8 7 6 5 4 3 2 1

Library of Congress Cataloging in Publication Data

Holt, James Clarke, comp.
    Magna carta and the idea of liberty.

    (Major issues in history)
    Bibliography: p.
    1. Magna carta—Addresses, essays, lectures.
2. Liberty—Addresses, essays, lectures. I. Title.
JN147.H643   323.44   70-38963
ISBN 0-471-40845-X
ISBN 0-471-40843-3 (pbk.)

SERIES PREFACE

The reading program in a history survey course traditionally has consisted of a large two-volume textbook and, perhaps, a book of readings. This simple reading program requires few decisions and little imagination on the instructor's part, and tends to encourage in the student the virtue of careful memorization. Such programs are by no means things of the past, but they certainly do not represent the wave of the future.

The reading program in survey courses at many colleges and universities today is far more complex. At the risk of oversimplification, and allowing for many exceptions and overlaps, it can be divided into four categories: (1) textbook, (2) original source readings, (3) specialized historical essays and interpretive studies, and (4) historical problems.

After obtaining an overview of the course subject matter (textbook), sampling the original sources, and being exposed to selective examples of excellent modern historical writing (historical essays), the student can turn to the crucial task of weighing various possible interpretations of major historical issues. It is at this point that memory gives way to creative critical thought. The "problems approach," in other words, is the intellectual climax of a thoughtfully conceived reading program and is, indeed, the most characteristic of all approaches to historical pedagogy among the newer generation of college and university teachers.

The historical problems books currently available are many and varied. Why add to this information explosion? Because the Wiley Major Issues Series constitutes an endeavor to produce something new that will respond to pedagogical needs thus far unmet. First, it is a series of individual volumes—one per problem. Many good teachers would much prefer to select their own historical issues rather than be tied to an inflexible sequence of issues imposed by a publisher and bound together between two covers. Second, the Wiley Major Issues Series is based on the idea of approaching the significant problems of history through a deft interweaving of primary sources and secondary analysis, fused together by the skill of a scholar-editor. It is felt that the essence of a historical issue cannot be satisfactorily probed either by placing a body of undigested source materials into the hands of inexperienced students or by limiting these students to the controversial literature of modern scholars who debate the meaning of sources the student never sees. This series approaches historical problems by exposing students to both the finest historical thinking on the issue and some of the evidence on which this thinking is based. This synthetic approach should prove far more fruitful than either the raw-source approach or the exclusively second-hand approach, for it combines the advantages—and avoids the serious disadvantage—of both.

Finally, the editors of the individual volumes in the Major Issues Series have been chosen from among the ablest scholars in their fields. Rather than faceless referees, they are historians who know their issues from the inside and, in most instances, have themselves contributed significantly to the relevant scholarly literature. It has been the editorial policy of this series to permit the editor-scholars of the individual volumes the widest possible latitude both in formulating their topics and in organizing their materials. Their scholarly competence has been unquestioningly respected; they have been encouraged to approach the problems as they see fit. The titles and themes of the series volumes have been suggested in nearly every case by the scholar-editors themselves. The criteria have been (1) that the issue be of relevance to undergraduate lecture courses in history, and (2) that it be an issue which the scholar-editor knows thoroughly and in which he has done creative work. And, in general, the second criterion has been given precedence over the first. In short, the question "What are the significant historical issues today?" has been answered not by general editors or sales departments but by the scholar-teachers who are responsible for these volumes.

University of California,   *C. Warren Hollister*
Santa Barbara

CONTENTS

INTRODUCTION

Medieval states reveal with unusual clarity two stresses that occur in any form of society. One is the conflict between government initiative and established law; the other is the rivalry between those in and out of office. In medieval times the first turned on the king's power to invent new administrative or financial procedures; the second on the exercise of royal patronage. Under a "good" king and in easy circumstances these stresses were absorbed without difficulty; law was changed by agreed and traditional procedures, the king worked along accepted customary lines, office was distributed in such a way that powerful interests were not irremediably alienated. Under a "bad" king or in difficult circumstances these stresses led to political crisis, and perhaps to rebellion. They were never entirely separate; "bad" government was invariably associated with "bad" officials and courtiers; but each produced its characteristic form of opposition. The conflict about patronage led to demands that the rewards of loyal service should be confined to natives, or that traditional aristocratic office should be given a real role in government or, in extreme circumstances, to schemes for the control of the king by an aristocratic council managed by a rebellious faction. The conflict about law led to statements of ancient custom in the form of "constitutions" or "establishments," or to a demand for charters of liberties in which the king granted rights and privileges to his subjects. Of these Magna Carta was the most enduring and the most famous.

Such charters occupy an important and clearly defined place in the development of the relations between the individual and the state. In reality they were exacted from the king by force, or the threat of force, or by bargaining support. Nevertheless, they

1

always took the form of freely given grants; anything less would
have impugned them at birth. Hence they provided a method of
defining and guaranteeing the rights of subjects without at the
same time raising the whole question of the ultimate source of
authority within the state. They also had the advantage that they
took a familiar form used in everyday transactions for the con-
veyancing of land or the transfer of rights from one individual to
another. They had their heyday between the middle of the
twelfth and the middle of the fourteenth century; there were of
course some outliers, both earlier, notably the charter of liberties
of Henry I of England, 1100, and later, in particular a number of
charters issued in the Low Countries and in Germany; but essentially they belong to the High Middle Ages. From the sixteenth
century they came to be superseded by other forms drawn from
notions of natural rights and social contract; these took shape as
statements of parliamentary liberties or as revolutionary declarations of rights or both.

The Great Charter exacted from King John at Runnymede in
June 1215 is a good example of the *genre,* both in content and
in the circumstances from which it sprang. It marked the culmination of a crisis to which there were many contributory causes:
the rapid growth of royal government in England under Henry
II (1154–1189), Richard I (1189–1199), and John (1199–1216);
the increasingly severe financial strain imposed by the need to
defend the widespread possessions of Henry II's house in France;
the failure of these policies culminating in the loss of Normandy
and other provinces to the French in 1204–1206; the breakdown
of relationships with the Papacy, with all its attendant diplomatic
disadvantages, as a result of a dispute over an election to the
Archbishopric of Canterbury, 1205–1213; the increasingly objectionable "tyranny" of King John, marked by his keen personal
interest in the government of England, his readiness to distort
normal feudal relationships into sources of royal revenue and instruments of political discipline, and his reliance on a relatively
small group of favored agents and supporters, including castellans
and sheriffs drawn from Normandy and Poitou; and finally the
disastrous failure of John's attempt to reconquer the lost provinces in France in a campaign in 1214 in which his Flemish and
German allies and some of his own men were decisively defeated
at Bouvines on July 27. The charter was not simply a negative

response to these developments. It also drew on ideas about government and law which were in part a product of the schools, in part drawn from more developed notions of feudal contract, in part derived from the theory and practice of common law as they had developed in England during the reigns of Henry II and his sons.

Such a document provoked a wide range of responses at the time. The baronial party which had won the charter claimed that it was a statement of the law of the realm (no. 1). The King's supporters on the other hand argued that it was an unwarrantable intrusion into the traditional rights of the Crown (no. 2). Still others viewed the charter not as some great statement of law but rather as an attempt to secure purely feudal privileges in the interests of the nobility (no. 3). These divisions of opinion have continued down to the present day; examples are given below from the seventeenth century (nos. 4, 5) and from historical work ranging over the last hundred years (nos. 7, 8, 9, 10). Moreover, the charter survived through many centuries as a vital legal and political document, so that later views of it have often involved more than simple differences of historical interpretation; they have amounted to serious, sometimes fundamental differences on the issues of the day. Hence part of the conflict between the common law and the royal prerogative in the seventeenth century depended on the interpretation of certain crucial sections in the charter; so also did the complaints of the American colonists against the government of George III, and so also did the arguments of English radicals, both in the seventeenth and nineteenth centuries, against what they regarded as an intolerable attack by Parliament on the fundamental liberties of the subject. These developments are noteworthy in two respects. First, it is by no means obvious why men should continue to look back to an antiquated feudal document as a justification for legal and political arguments. Why continue to appeal to Magna Carta, why continue to interpret or distort its original content instead of devising some new guarantee of liberty? It was not until the seventeenth century that its position was even rivalled by the Petition and Bill of Rights, and then only to leave these three, as the Earl of Chatham put it, as "the Bible of the English Constitution." Second, it is far from clear why this should happen in England alone. Some other European liberties enjoyed a rela-

tively long life. The Charter to the Normans granted in 1315 was
last confirmed by Louis XI in 1462 and survived as part of the
custom of Normandy until the Revolution (no. 20). The Golden
Bull of Hungary of 1222 had an even longer life for it was confirmed by successive Hungarian kings at their coronation down
to the end of the Hungarian monarchy (no. 19). Neither, however, played the role which the Great Charter played in England.
The Norman charter was provincial; the Golden Bull was used
as a formal defence of the constitutional position of the aristocracy. Moreover such survival was quite exceptional. Throughout
the rest of western Europe most charters of liberties had become
defunct or reduced to purely antiquarian significance by the ab-
solutist monarch of the sixteenth and seventeenth centuries and
their respectable counterparts, the "enlightened" despots of the
eighteenth century (no. 22).

There seem to be two obvious lines along which to try to
solve these problems. One is to study the charter's survival: first
the measures taken immediately afterwards to ensure its publication and enforcement, then the recurrent reinterpretations by
which it was kept up to date and applied to new situations. This
seam has been very fully worked by Miss Faith Thompson and
many others. It is illustrated, both in general and with particular
reference to the history of chapter 39, in nos. 11 to 15. The second line of approach is to ask whether there were features in the
original document which did something to ensure its survival.

Each approach has its own difficulties. Those of the first are
largely logical. There is not only the problem raised above of
explaining why men should interpret and "distort" an old document rather than design a new one. There is also a problem of
defining "reinterpretation" and "distortion" in the light of the
fact that the charter was designed as a grant in perpetuity, intended to last for all time. Moreover reinterpretation played its
most important role in the development of a small number of
chapters, foremost among which was chapter 39 (no. 12), which
were themselves drafted with some vagueness in the original
charter; they left room for different interpretations in the interests of political compromise. Finally distortion and reinterpretation does not represent some new political illness inflicted upon
the English body politic after 1215. True, the Charter was distorted by later generations, but it was itself a distortion of the

past in its implied claim that all its provisions represented good and ancient custom (nos. 10, 16). It was not only law but also propaganda. For all these reasons it is quite unrealistic to argue, for example, that a purely feudal concession in 1215 was changed solely by the ingenuity of later generations into a guarantee of individual liberty. The original charter and its subsequent history are quite inseparable. Helen Cam neatly summarized the resulting problem for the historian in her title "Magna Carta— Event or Document" (no. 15). "Magna Carta—Event *and* Document" might have been even more apposite.

The second approach is essentially comparative. If it is to be argued that in 1215 Magna Carta already had the qualities or at least the potentialities for survival then it must be established that these features were not shared elsewhere. This raises practical difficulties, for Magna Carta has been much more thoroughly studied than its continental counterparts. Many of these still await properly critical editions; in many cases too the subsequent history of the charters has only been followed sketchily. The present writer has been collecting the texts over a number of years in the hope of producing a critical edition of at least a selection. This search has led to the discovery not only of new versions of existing texts but also of charters of liberties hitherto unknown.

There is a further difficulty. The comparison of charters involves the comparison of the circumstances which produced them and of the factors which told for or against their survival as documents of political importance. These circumstances are more difficult to study than the charters themselves. There is no country in western Europe which can rival England in the surviving official records of the government and courts of law. Hence it is hazardous to seek an explanation of the charter's survival in some apparently unique features in English society of the time. True, arguments of some cogency can be advanced along these lines. England was small and relatively easily controlled by a strong central government. Hence Magna Carta was granted to all free men of the realm.[1] This was quite different from the situation in France in 1315 when Louis X's concessions were em-

---

[1] So the Charter asserts. Nevertheless the Earl of Chester granted a separate and distinct charter of liberties to his men of Cheshire.

bodied in a number of provincial charters which reinforced local privileges. Again, there is something to be said for the argument that English society was particularly cohesive and that the term "free man" as it figured in the charter had a special sense which it enjoyed in no other country. These and similar comparisons and contrasts are advanced in nos. 16, 17, 18, 21 and 23 below. Nos. 19 and 20, which consist of selections from the Golden Bull of Hungary and the Charter of the Normans, provide material for the reader's own comparisons.

This aspect of the problem is one which requires a great amount of study before it can be properly aligned with the mass of careful and detailed work on the subsequent history of the charter in England. It may be that the final answer will not be one based immediately on direct social contrasts between England and the continent. It is more likely that the solution will be found by relating charters of liberties to the development of law, legislation, and legal administration. There is much to be said for the argument that Magna Carta owed its long history to the fact that it coincided with, and partly arose from, a rapid development of the English legal system in which lawyers were searching for an effective vehicle for legislation. This was what the Charter provided. The result was that Magna Carta was embedded in the structure of law as the first English statute. In this England may well have been unique.[2]

Such comparisons are also relevant to the central argument about the charter. To denounce it as aristocratic and reactionary or to praise it as long-sighted and liberal is equally unsound. Both extremes go beyond common sense. Both contribute to an artificial conflict of opinion. Magna Carta is not necessarily deprived of long-lasting significance by demonstrating that the barons who fought for it were concerned with selfish ends; there is nothing new or unusual about that. Equally the long history of the charter does not necessarily mean that the men of 1215 were endowed with exceptional political insight. In the end the student is left with the problem of standards. What is to be understood by such terms as "reactionary," "muddled," "sensible," "constructive," or "unconstructive" when applied to the provi-

2 See J. C. Holt, "Magna Carta and the origin of Statute Law" in *Essays in Honour of Gaines Post (Studia Gratiana,* Bologna, 1972).

sions of these documents? No absolute answer is possible. It is rather a matter of comparisons: comparison of the provisions within each charter, and above all comparison of the provisions of different charters. In such an assessment Magna Carta does not always come off best; in no. 21 for example, a distinguished Spanish historian compares the security provisions of the 1215 version of the charter with those of Spanish liberties to the former's disadvantage. Nevertheless in general Magna Carta seems more sophisticated than the Hungarian liberties, less provincial than the French, more comprehensive than the Spanish, less aristocratic than the German. More than any other charter, it showed a close interest in the everyday working of government, the routine administration of justice and the detailed provisions of the common law. These contrasts are discussed incidentally or at length in nos. 9, 10, 16, 17, 18 and 23. They amount to a recipe for survival.

In this way the comparative method, though primarily concerned with the reasons for the charter's survival, leads back to the division of opinion which has left so great a mark on the historiography of the charter. It should be noted that this division has not only affected views about the charter. It has also cut deep into the general history of political thought; for, if charters of liberties are, as it were, to be set on one side as statements of feudal liberties and nothing more, then it becomes possible, perhaps even necessary, to draw a sharp distinction between the medieval idea of "liberties" and the modern notion of "Liberty," the one tied to status within the social or ecclesiastical hierarchy, the other to the natural right of the individual; the one arising from grave social inequality the other from equality of all adults in a free society.

This point of view is put forward with great force by A. F. Pollard in no. 24. It is open to two obvious lines of criticism. One would be concerned with the consequences of economic laissez-faire and the question whether liberty and equality are as mutually compatible as the argument assumes; it lies outside the scope of this book. The other is to treat liberty not so much as an attribute of individuals or classes but rather as the juridical capacity or legal competence to commit oneself freely to this or that. This book concludes with two statements of such a point of view advanced by Belgian scholars writing very much from

the jurist's standpoint (nos. 25, 26). Defined thus, the study of
liberty simply excludes much of Pollard's argument, for it does
not matter whether liberty is confined either to a small proportion of a given society or to limited number of actions within
that society. Nor is there any need to draw any distinction between "liberties" and "Liberty." The second simply grows out
of the first.

Such an approach requires care. It may very easily slide into a
series of anachronistic interpretations which remove the provisions of these charters from their contemporary context and subject them to entirely artificial a priori reasoning. On the other
hand it does allow for the long, almost continuous development
which Magna Carta underwent down to the seventeenth century
and beyond. And it does accept that even medieval charters of
liberties may state durable political principles.

These are the broad terms of the debate about Magna Carta
and similar documents. To summarize, it is obvious, first, that
charters of liberties are concerned with the political stresses of
contemporary societies. Secondly, some of these stresses were
purely temporary; hence these charters are concerned with feudal
matters like reliefs, wardship, and rights of marriage which are
of little permanent importance. Thirdly, some of the conflicts
that the charters were intended to solve arose from continuing
political problems like the rights of subjects in legal process and
the powers of governments in making law or invading property.
Fourthly, some charters stated positions in such matters that were
of continuing interest to later generations. Finally, the extent to
which this happened depended not only on such an interest but
also on the local circumstances, especially the development of
law and the nature of the social structure, which determined the
quality of the initial grant and gave it greater or less potentiality
for the future.

The student who approaches the history of Magna Carta for
the first time in this book will find it helpful to remember the
following sequence of the documents:

1.   Magna Carta was based on a preliminary agreement sealed
by King John which stated the baronial demands as petitions.
This agreement still survives in the British Museum and is
known from its endorsement as the *Articles* or the *Article of the
Barons*. It is undated but probably belongs to June 10, 1215.

2.   Magna Carta 1215 is dated June 15, but final peace was not agreed between the King and the barons until June 19. This is the longest version of the charter. It was legally valid only for a few months in the summer of 1215 and was formerly annulled by papal bull of August 24, 1215 (no. 2) which reached England at the end of September.

The text of Magna Carta 1215 is given in the Appendix. It included a number of chapters which were later regarded as "grave and doubtful" and also several provisions which were solely concerned with John's government and had less importance once he was dead (October 19, 1216). All these chapters were excluded from later versions; they are marked with an asterisk in the text in the Appendix.

3.   The first reissue of November 12, 1216 was an interim measure. It included little new material but excluded the "grave and doubtful" chapters mentioned above.

4.   The second reissue of September/November 1217 was intended to be a definitive version. A considerable amount of new material was added in this version which also included detailed amendments to the original provisions of 1215. Little was done at this stage to bring back the chapters excluded in 1216. However, the Charter of Liberties was now supplemented by a comprehensive Charter of the Forest, dated November 6, 1217. This was concerned with the extent of the royal forest and the regulation of the forest law. Henceforth the two charters were confirmed and reissued together.

5.   The final reissue of February 11, 1225 included only minor verbal amendments to the text of 1217, except in the final chapter which now stated that the charter was conceded of the King's free will in return for the grant of a subsidy. The text of 1225 became the definitive text in the thirteenth century. It was this text which was confirmed in Edward I's *Confirmation of the Charters* of 1297. Edward's confirmation was enrolled on the Statute Roll; it is the statutory text, identified as 25 Edward I, to which all subsequent legislation refers.

It is important to remember that some of the most striking features of the 1215 Charter, in particular the proposals for the assessment of certain forms of taxation by consent (caps. 12 and 14) and the arrangements for a court or committee of twenty-five barons to supervise the execution of the Charter (cap. 61), were not included in the later issues. Nevertheless there is occasional confusion. The various texts of the charter were not properly distinguished until Blackstone's *Great Charter* of 1759 (no. 6); hence some seventeenth century commentators discuss chapters of the 1215 Charter as part of the law of the land even though they never figured in the subsequent reissues.

Finally no historical problem can be studied effectively without acquiring the appropriate vocabulary. No attempt has been made below to explain such terms as *fee, feof* or *fief,* which are common to medieval history as a whole. However, the study of charters of liberties does necessarily confront the student with a number of technical terms peculiar to the subject. These have been included in the Glossary. Terms that only figure occasionally have been explained in the footnotes to the text.

PART ONE

The Debate About Magna Carta

CONTEMPORARY APPRAISALS

1 FROM *Mandate from Geoffrey de Mandeville, earl of Essex and Gloucester, Saer de Quenci, earl of Winchester, and Richard de Clare, earl of Hertford, to Brian de Lisle, custodian of Knaresborough Castle, September 30, 1215*

Magna Carta 1215 cap. 61 established a body of Twenty Five barons who were to supervise the execution of the charter and deal with complaints against the king. They were empowered to compel him to accept their judgment.

This mandate is concerned with such a case. Knaresborough castle had been surrendered to the King by Nicholas de Stuteville as part of a fine agreed with the King for the succession to his nephew's estates in 1205. In 1215 he attempted recovery by appealing to the judgment of the Twenty Five; the mandate illustrates the execution of such a judgment under the terms of caps. 55 and 61 of Magna Carta. It also reveals baronial attitudes to the charter itself.

The mandate is issued by three of the twenty-five and is witnessed by a fourth.

Geoffrey de Mandeville, earl of Essex and Gloucester, Saer de Quenci, earl of Winchester, and Richard de Clare, earl of Hert-

SOURCE. London, Public Record Office, Ancient Petitions, no. 15693. Reprinted by permission of the Controller of Her Majesty's Stationery Office.

ford to Brian de Lisle, greeting. We order you that, on receipt of these letters, you are to hold to the oath which you have given to follow the charter to the commune of the realm and restore the castle of Knaresborough to Nicholas de Stuteville; for it has been adjudged to him as his right by the Twenty Five barons. If you do not do this, have no further trust in us, either as regards your person or your lands or your chattels, for all those who contravene this judgment and this mandate, are against the judgment and law of the realm. Witness, Robert de Vere, earl of Oxford, at London on the 30th day of September in the year of the Incarnation of our Lord 1215.

2   FROM   *The Bull* Etsi Karissimus *of Pope Innocent III, annulling Magna Carta, August 24, 1215*

King John sought papal annulment of Magna Carta by the middle of July 1215. Both King and barons had earlier appealed for papal arbitration. The Pope sided with John, who had been his vassal since the settlement of the quarrel with Rome in July 1213. In the Bull, Innocent reviewed the course of the negotiations and then in this passage pronounced the annulment.

When the archbishop and bishops would not take any action, seeing himself bereft of almost all counsel and help, he did not dare to refuse what the barons had dared to demand. And so by such violence and fear as might affect the most courageous of men he was forced to accept an agreement which is not only shameful and demeaning but also illegal and unjust, thereby lessening unduly and impairing his royal rights and dignity.

SOURCE. C. R. Cheney and W. H. Semple, *Selected Letters of Innocent III*, London, 1953, pp. 215–6. Reprinted by permission of Thomas Nelson & Sons Ltd.

But because the Lord has said to us by the prophet Jeremiah, "I have set thee over the nations and over the kingdoms, to root out, and to destroy, to build and to plant,"[1] and also by Isaiah, "Loose the bands of wickedness, undo the heavy burden,"[2] we refuse to ignore such shameless presumption, for thereby the Apostolic See would be dishonoured, the king's rights injured, the English nation shamed, and the whole plan for a Crusade seriously endangered; and as this danger would be imminent if concessions, thus extorted from a great prince who has taken the cross,[3] were not cancelled by our authority, even though he himself should prefer them to be upheld, on behalf of Almighty God, Father, Son, and Holy Spirit, and by the authority of Saints Peter and Paul His apostles, and by our own authority, acting on the general advice of our brethren, we utterly reject and condemn this settlement, and under threat of excommunication we order that the king should not dare to observe it and that the barons and their associates should not require it to be observed. the charter, with all undertakings and guarantees whether confirming it or resulting from it, we declare to be null, and void of all validity for ever. Wherefore, let no man deem it lawful to infringe this document of our annulment and prohibition, or presume to oppose it. If anyone should presume to do so, let him know that he will incur the anger of Almighty God and of Saints Peter and Paul His apostles.

Anagni, the 24th of August, in the eighteenth year of our Pontificate.

[1] Jeremiah, 1: 9–10.

[2] Isaiah, 58: 6.

[3] John took the Cross on March 4, 1215 in order to seal his alliance with the papacy and in the hope of staving off rebellion.

3   FROM   *The History of the Dukes of*
                Normandy and Kings of England

*This chronicle, written in French, is the work of an anonymous
writer who accompanied John's Flemish allies to England in
1215. He gives a contemporary and firsthand narrative of the
last eighteen months of John's reign. His account is of considerable interest, especially since it is not monastic in origin; nevertheless, it is not partisan for King John.*

The king went to Staines and there he had to accept such
terms as the barons wished. He was forced to agreè that a woman
should never be married so that she would be disparaged; this
was the best agreement which he made with them, had it been
well kept. In addition he had to agree that he would never cause
a man to lose life or limb for any wild beast that he took,[1] but
that he should be able to pay a fine. These two things could
easily be borne. He had to fix reliefs for land, which had been
excessive, at such a figure as they wished. They wished to have
all powers of high justice throughout their lands. And they demanded many other things, with good reason, of which I make
no mention. Above all this they wanted Twenty-Five barons to
be chosen so that the king should treat them in all matters by
the judgment of these Twenty-Five. He would redress through
these all the wrongs he did them and they likewise would redress
through these all the wrongs they did him. And they also wished
that the king would not appoint any bailiff anywhere in his land
except through the Twenty-Five.[2] The king agreed to all this by
force, and for the observance of this peace gave his charter to the
barons as one who could do no other.

[1] This provision is not in Magna Carta 1215. It is included in the Charter
of the Forest, 1217.

[2] This provision is not in Magna Carta 1215, but compare caps. 45, 50.

SOURCE. *Histoire des Ducs de Normandie et des Rois d'Angleterre*, ed.
Francisque Michel (Société de l'Histoire de France, 1840), pp. 149–50.

THE SEVENTEENTH CENTURY
ARGUMENT

4 FROM   *Sir Edward Coke*
The First Part of the Institutes of the Laws
of England, 1628

Edward Coke (1552–1634), Chief Justice of the Common Pleas 1606, Chief Justice of the King's Bench, 1613. Suspended and dismissed by King James I in 1616, he became the apostle of the common law against the royal prerogative. The First Institute takes the form of a commentary on Sir Thomas Littleton's (1422–1481) Treatise on Tenures and is sometimes described as "Coke on Littleton."

This parliamentary charter hath divers appellations in law. Here it is called Magna Carta, not for the length or largeness of it (for it is but those in respect of the charters granted of private things to private persons nowadays being) but it is called the Great Charter in respect of the great weightiness and weighty greatness of the matter contained in it in few words,[1] being the fountain of all the fundamental Laws of the Realm, and therefore it may truly be said of it that it is "great matter in small

---

[1] This assessment was influential, even though false. The charter was called "Great" to distinguish it from the companion Charter of the Forest.

SOURCE: Edward Coke, *The first Part of the Institutes of the Laws of England,* London, 1628, Book 2, Chapter 2, Section 108.

content."[2] It is in our books called "Charter of Liberties and the Common Liberty of England," or "the Liberties of England," "the Charter of Liberties," "Magna Carta" etc. And well may the Laws of England be called liberties because they make free men.[3] And great was once the reverence of this great charter.

This statute of Magna Carta, is but a confirmation or restitution of the Common Law, as in the statute called the Confirmation of the Charters it appeareth by the opinion of all the Justices. . .[4]

This statute of Magna Carta hath been confirmed above thirty times, and commanded to be put in execution. By the statute of 25 Edward I cap. 2[5] judgments given against any points of the Charters of Magna Carta or the Charter of the Forest are adjudged void, and by the Statute of 42 Edward III, cap. 3, if any statute be made against either of these charters it shall be void.[6]

5   FROM   *Robert Brady*
Introduction to the old English History, 1684

Robert Brady, d. 1700, Master of Caius College, Cambridge 1660, Fellow of the Royal College of Physicians and physician in ordinary to both Charles II and James II, M.P. for Cambridge 1681 and 1685, a high Tory and polemical defender of the royal prerogative. Brady was also a serious student of historical sources

[2] Coke's phrase is more succinct in his Latin—*magnum in parvo.*

[3] Again Coke's Latin is more telling—"called *libertates quia liberos faciunt.*"

[4] The Confirmation of the Charters of Edward I, 1297. Coke seems to refer to cap. 1, which compels the justices to observe the charter in the courts of common law.

[5] The Confirmation of the Charters, 1297.

[6] This is one of the points of origin of a lengthy debate on the relationship of fundamental law, especially as expressed in the Great Charter, to parliamentary sovereignty. The problem is reviewed in J. W. Gough, *Fundamental Law in English Constitutional History,* Oxford, 1961, pp. 12–47.

SOURCE: Robert Brady, *An Introduction to the old English History,* London, 1684, p. 76.

*and an informed critic of the arguments which exploited medi-
eval precedent against the Crown; "in that he treated his texts
as the product of the medieval past and sought to discover their
meaning to the men who wrote them, his work has remained of
permanent importance after its polemical significance has evap-
orated."*[1]

For the far greatest part of Magna Carta concerned tenants in
military service only, and the Liberties, which our ancient historians tell were so mightily contended for, if seriously considered, were mainly the Liberties of Holy Church, by which, in
most things, she pretended to be free from subjection to a temporal prince; and the relaxation of the original rigour upon
which knights', or military, fees were first given by the lords, and
accepted by the tenants.

[1] D. C. Douglas, *English Scholars 1660–1730*, London, 1951, p. 124.

SOME MODERN VIEWS

6 FROM   *William Blackstone*
The Great Charter and the Charter of the Forest, 1759

*Sir William Blackstone, 1723–80, first professor of English law
in the University of Oxford 1758–66, Justice of the Common
Pleas, 1770, author of* Commentaries on the Laws of England,
1765–9.

*The modern study of Magna Carta begins with Blackstone.
Hitherto, lawyers, scholars, and politicians had relied on texts
derived either from the* Greater Chronicle of Matthew Paris,
*printed by Parker in 1585, or the confirmation of 25 Edward I
(1297). The first confuses the text of the Charter of 1215 with
that of the reissue of 1225 and also includes apocryphal chapters
which have survived only in the St. Albans chronicles;[1] the second confirms the charter of Henry III of 1225. Blackstone was
the first scholar to study and collate the surviving original
charters and to distinguish properly between the different versions. His edition is a classic and even now requires very little
amendment.*

There is no transaction in the ancient part of our English
history more interesting and important, than the rise and

[1] See J. C. Holt, "The St. Albans Chroniclers and Magna Carta." *Transactions of the Royal Historical Society*, V. 14 (1964), pp. 67–88.

SOURCE. William Blackstone, *The Great Charter and the Charter of the
Forest*, Oxford, 1759, p. i.

progress, the gradual mutation, and final establishment of the charters of liberties, emphatically styled the Great Charter and Charter of the Forest; and yet there is none that has been transmitted down to us with less accuracy and historical precision. There is not hitherto extant any full and correct copy of the charter granted by king John, Mr. Pine's engraving excepted,[2] which, on account of the antiquity of its character, is not fitted for general perusal: and the charters of king Henry the third have always been printed, even in our statute-books, not from the originals themselves, but from an *Inspeximus* of king Edward the first. This want of authentic materials, or neglect of recurring to such as might be easily had, (of which the foregoing are two very glaring instances) has often betrayed our very best historians and most painful antiquarians into gross and palpable errors, as will in some measure appear from the following deduction; to adjust and remedy which, as well as our remaining evidence and the distance of five centuries will allow, is the principal end of the present publication.

7 FROM   *William Stubbs*
   The Constitutional History of England, 1897

William Stubbs (1825–1901), Regius Professor of Modern History in the University of Oxford 1866–1884, bishop of Oxford 1888–1901. Stubb's interpretation of the charter set the pattern for a whole generation of scholars. However, in his emphasis on the emergence of the "nation" and on the "national" or "popular" character of chartered liberties, he expressed views which were generally current among "liberal" historians in the generation be-

[2] John Pine 1690–1756, engraver. Pine's engraving of 1733 was of one of the original charters of 1215 preserved in the Cottonian Library. The original had been damaged in the fire of the Cottonian Library of 1731; words were replaced from the second original surviving in that library.

SOURCE. W. Stubbs, *Constitutional History of England*, 6th edition, Oxford 1896–1897, vol. 1, pp. 569–572.

fore and immediately after World War I. Stubbs was a powerful influence in perpetuating these notions; his formidable scholarship and extraordinary breadth of mind have ensured the survival of his work even though some of the political and philosophical assumptions it expresses may now seem outmoded.

The Great Charter, although drawn up in the form of a royal grant, was really a treaty between the king and his subjects; it was framed upon a series of articles drawn up by them, it contained the provision usual in treaties for securing its execution, and, although in express terms it contained only one part of the covenant, it implied in its whole tenour the existence and recognition of the other. The king granted these privileges on the understanding that he was to retain the allegiance of the nation. It is the collective people who really form the other high contracting party in the great capitulation,—the three estates of the realm, not it is true arranged in order according to their profession or rank, but not the less certainly combined in one national purpose, and securing by one bond the interests and rights of each other severally and of all together. The Charter contains a clause similar to that by which Henry I tried to secure the rights of his subjects as against the mesne lords; but now the provision is adopted by the lords themselves for the security of fair and equal justice: "All the aforesaid customs and liberties that we have granted to be held in our kingdom so far as pertains to us, with reference to our vassals, all men of our kingdom, as well clerk as lay, shall observe, so far as pertains to them, with reference to their men."[1] The barons maintain and secure the right of the whole people as against themselves as well as against their master. Clause by clause the rights of the commons are provided for as well as the rights of the nobles; the interest of the freeholder is everywhere coupled with that of the barons and knights; the stock of the merchant and the wainage of the villein are preserved from undue severity of amercement as well as the settled estate of the earldom or barony.[2] The knight is protected against the

[1] Cap. 60.
[2] Cap. 20.

compulsory exaction of his services, and the horse and cart of the freeman against the irregular requisition even of the sheriff.[3] In every case in which the privilege of the simple freeman is not secured by the provision that primarily affects the knight or baron, a supplementary clause is added to define and protect his right; and the whole advantage is obtained for him by the comprehensive article which closes the essential part of the charter.

This proves, if any proof were wanted, that the demands of the barons were no selfish exaction of privilege for themselves; it proves with scarcely less certainty that the people for whom they acted were on their side. The nation in general, the people of the towns and villages, the commons of later days, the Englishmen who had fought the battles of the Norman kings against the feudatories, had now thrown themselves on the side of the barons: John's tyranny had overthrown that balance of the powers of the state which his predecessors had striven with so much earnestness and so much policy to adjust. We do not indeed find, in the list of those who forced the king to yield, any names that prove the commons to have been influential in the drawing up of the articles: the conspicuous names are those of the northern barons, of the men of the great ministerial houses, and of that remnant of the Conqueror's baronage that had cut themselves loose from Normandy and Norman principles and reconciled themselves to the nobler position of leaders of their brother Englishmen. It was probably by the bishops, Langton[4] in particular, and the legal members of the confederacy, that the rights of the freeholder were so carefully fenced round with provisions. These men and their successors led the commons and acted for them until the Reformation, with little discord and still less jealousy of their rising influence; and it was the extinction of the class which furnished their natural leaders that threw the Church and the nation under the tyranny that followed the Wars of the Roses.

The Great Charter is the first great public act of the nation, after it has realised its own identity: the consummation of the work for which unconsciously kings, prelates, and lawyers have been labouring for a century. There is not a word in it that recalls the distinctions of race and blood, or that maintains the differ-

3 Caps. 16, 29, 30.
4 Stephen Langton, archbishop of Canterbury, 1206–1228.

ences of English and Norman law. It is in one view the summing up of a period of national life, in another the starting-point of a new period, not less eventful than that which it closes.

Magna Carta in its completed form attests the account given by the historians of its origin and growth. It is based on the charter of Henry I; it follows the arrangement of that famous document, and it amplifies and expands it, so as to bring under the principles, which were for the first time laid down in A.D. 1100, all the particular rights, claims, and duties which had come into existence during the development of the intervening century. . . . the whole of the constitutional history of England is little more than a commentary on Magna Carta.

8 FROM *Edward Jenks*
The Myth of Magna Carta, 1902

Edward Jenks, 1861–1939, professor of law at Melbourne, Liverpool and London, author of Law and Politics in the Middle Ages, *1898. Jenks was simply Brady to Stubbs's Coke; just as Brady attacked the common-law myth of ancient law expressed in chartered liberties, so Jenks attacked the "national" liberties of Stubbs's school; both Brady and Jenks pleaded for a "feudal" interpretation of the charter. Jenks's paper, the whole of which is reproduced here, still remains the most extreme expression of this point of view.*

"Magna Carta is then the first corporate act of the nation roused to the sense of its unity." "The nation in general, the people of the towns and villages, the commons of later days . . . had now thrown themselves on the side of the barons." "The people . . . for the first time since the Conquest ranged themselves on the side of the barons against the king."

SOURCE. E. Jenks, "The Myth of Magna Carta," *Independent Review*, vol. 4, 1902, pp. 260–273.

These are the words, clear and unmistakeable, of a writer to whom every student of English history owes an incalculable debt, who combines great learning with sound judgment, who is, in fact, almost above praise, whose memory is one of the precious things of those who were privileged to sit at his feet. The view which the words express, though he did not found it, has passed into modern text-books written under his influence—has, in fact, become classical, accepted alike by scholars and laymen. Though, in a sense, but an abstract view, it cannot be regarded, surely, as of interest only to experts; for, if it be true, the grant of Magna Carta was an epoch in the national life, if it be untrue, the whole nation is being trained to take a distorted view of its own past.

Clear and unmistakeable are the words. They assert, that the Great Charter was the result, not of a class movement, still less of an accidental conspiracy, but of the united efforts of "the nation, the people of the towns and villages"—in fact, of all ranks in the community. The Charter was not merely won *for* "the people"; it was won *by* "the people," in conjunction, of course, with the barons and the prelates.

This is a momentous fact, if it be a fact. Happily, the evidence by which it must stand or fall, is neither obscure nor technical, and can be appreciated by the layman almost as well as by the historical expert. It is only necessary for us to put aside preconceived notions, and look at the testimony. All the beliefs of past generations cannot make a conclusion true, if the evidence does not warrant it.

Shall the expected word of apology here be said? By one at least, and he most entitled, we may be very sure that no apology would have been desired. In his clear zeal for the truth, the late Bishop of Oxford would have welcomed every honest questioning of his conclusions. Never was a writer whose works breathe a purer spirit of devotion to the light; never one more patient of differing views, more earnest to foster the spirit of enquiry. Towards the writers who have reproduced his words, apology is less due; but it is freely offered. The general reader, impatient of attempts to disparage the equator, and incredulous of criticism, may be reminded, that other traditions, once very much accepted, have disappeared. Where is now the "folkland" of the Saxon nation? Where the "English Canon Law" of the days before the Reformation?

To come to the point. Till a few months ago, the writer held (and, it is to be feared, taught) the accepted view of Magna Carta, relying on the orthodox guides. A careful examination of the evidence, undertaken in discharge of a public duty, has slowly brought him to the conclusion, that there is no shadow of justification for the conventional doctrine—that in truth, Magna Carta was not (*a*) the work of the "nation" or the "people" in any reasonable sense of the term, nor (*b*) a landmark in constitutional progress, but (*c*) a positive nuisance and stumbling-block to the generation which came after it. In other words, it is "Great" only as the caravan giant is great, not as Napoleon and Goethe were great. It is a bulky document.

(*a*) Now the first of these three contentions is partly a matter of evidence, partly a matter of inference. Needless to say, the Charter itself affords no direct evidence for the view that it was won by the united efforts of "the people." Though addressed "to all the king's faithful men," it expressly bears to have been granted on the counsel of twenty-seven persons named, every one of whom was a prelate, an earl, or (as the Charter itself puts it), a noble; and the formal addition of "other faithful men of ours" must, according to the well-known rule of *ejusdem generis*, be held to mean, other men of a similar rank. Moreover, the Charter entrusts the execution of itself to a committee of "barons of the kingdom"; and, when these are chosen, their names are seen, with the single exception of that of the Mayor of London (of whom more hereafter) to be of the bluest blood of the feudal and official aristocracy.

But, of course, our knowledge of the circumstances is not confined to the Charter itself. Like almost all historical events, it was the outcome of both general and special causes. The former are known to all students of history; the latter are detailed for us in the writings of some score of chroniclers, several of them strictly contemporary, others living within a generation of the events which they describe.

The general cause at work, the cosmic force behind the framers of the Charter, was jealousy of the growing power of the monarchy. The twelfth century had been an age of great rulers. Frederick Barbarossa and Frederick II. in Germany, Philip Augustus in France, above all, Henry fitz Empress in England, had borne hardly upon feudal independence. The royal courts had tempted suitors away from the courts of the barony and the manor; the royal mints had threatened to abolish private coinage; the royal faces had been set like flints against the cherished right of private war. At the beginning of the twelfth century, the France of Louis the Fat had been a mere strip of land in the valley of the Seine and the Orléanais; at the beginning of the thirteenth, the iron hand of Philip Augustus ruled from Arras to Limoges, and from Burgundy to the rocks of Finisterre. As the twelfth century turned on its pivot, the English barons had been revelling in the licence which Stephen could not check; when the fourth quarter of the century was reached, they had known something of the "demon" power and serpentine cunning of Henry of Anjou. Above these earthly monarchs, gradually putting forward claims which, to the Europe of two centuries before, would have sounded fantastic, rose the mighty power of the Papacy, just now reaching its zenith in the person of Innocent III., "the greatest of all the successors of St. Peter." Innocent III. is a name not unknown in connection with Magna Carta; and it is worth noting that, the moment his own claims are acknowledged by John, his heavy hand is laid in the scale in favour of the King. Small wonder that a class which cherished memories of the days when every baron was king on his own land, should regard with dismay this new condition of things, should seek for an opportunity of revolt.

The reign of John was its golden opportunity. Of doubtful title, more than suspected of parricide, defeated and disgraced in war, entangled in a quarrel with the Pope from which he could only extricate himself by a shameful surrender, the King seemed born to afford his barons the chance for which they pined. As if to insist on his own destruction, John must needs heap personal insults on the natural leaders of a baronial revolt. The tale of his evil deeds is too well known to need repetition. Doubtless he did not spare the common people, if they came in his way; but his choicest insults were reserved for the bishops and abbots, whose churches he defaced and whose wool he seized, and for the nobles, whose wives and daughters he boastfully dishonoured. What wonder that his magnates turned upon him?

All this is clear beyond measure in the chronicles. But of any popular rising against the King, not one word. Gervase of Canterbury, Walter of Coventry, Bartholomew Cotton, Roger of Wendover, Henry of Knighton, Ralph of Coggeshall, Matthew of

Westminster, annalists of Burton, Margan, Tewkesbury, Winton, Waverley, Dunstable, Osney, Worcester—surely one of these would have had something to say of a popular rising? No. Everything is done by the "magnates," the "nobles," the "earls and barons," the *proceres,* the "knights"; it is almost impossible to reproduce the wearisome re-iteration of these terms by all the chroniclers. Not that these writers have any lack of words to describe the "people," when such is their desire. They can and do talk much of "burgesses," "husbandmen," "men of all sorts and conditions," "inhabitants." Sometimes these persons are being plundered, sometimes apologising to a legate for a hasty ebullition of lynching, sometimes hearing a charter read out by the sheriff. But of joining the baronial agitation, not one word. Much capital has been made out of the undoubted fact that London was long in the hands of the barons, and that its mayor was one of the executors of the Charter. But the actual accounts (especially that of Roger of Wendover), make it clear that the barons got possession of the city by a trick, through the connivance of a few of the wealthier citizens. The poorer sort were, in fact, for the King; and had to be roughly used to prevent them attacking the barons. One genuine "popular" rising the chroniclers do indeed show us, that of William, or Wilkin, in Sussex. And this was directed *against* the French allies of the barons. In fact, Matthew of Westminster seems to put the whole thing in a nutshell, when he describes the people of the eastern counties as being "miserably crushed as it were between two millstones rolling in reverse ways, to wit, the barons and the royalists." Surely an odd way for national heroes to behave.

This curious omission on the part of the chroniclers did not fail to strike so thorough a student as Dr. Stubbs.

"That the historians have recorded less of the action of the third estate, is accounted for by the fact, that at this period, and from this period to the Reformation, the baronage acts as advocate for it." . . . . "We do not indeed find, in the list of those who forced the King to yield, any names that prove the commons to have been influential in drawing up the articles."

These are damaging admissions; and they do not stand alone in Dr. Stubbs' works. Whether the baronage really did "act as advocate" for the commons, may well be doubted. We must consider that question at the next stage. But, in any case, advocacy is not co-operation; and it is co-operation which Dr. Stubbs, in the passages quoted at the head of this article, has emphatically asserted, and which his followers, less cautious than he, have alleged in still wider terms. In fact, at one point, the Bishop of Oxford seems to have almost abandoned his main contention; for he admits that, in the stormy opening of the drama, during the years 1208–13, we notice "the absence of anything like popular rebellion, and the postponement of the general rising to the end of the religious struggle." And he elsewhere hints, that this submission was purchased, in the earlier stages of the struggle, by a suspension of general taxation. Without entirely admitting the soundness of the reason, we may well admit the truth of the fact. But, once more we ask, where is the evidence for the "general rising at the end of the religious struggle"? Why had the barons to fight for almost every town which they held? Why, when John had been beaten and disgraced, did Tonbridge, Belvoir, Rockingham, Berkhampstead, York, and Hertford fall again into his hands? Why were forty of the leading barons themselves at the point of surrender when John died? Of course everyone knows the cock-and-bull story of the alleged treachery of the French. But that brings us to a still more formidable objection. *Why was it necessary for the barons to call in the French at all?* Surely it was an odd step for a party which at first put the banishment of foreigners in the forefront of its programme? The answer to all these questions is simple and obvious. The baronial party had no popular feeling behind it. In fact, there is some evidence to show that such faint popular manifestation as appeared, was on the side of the king.

(b) But let us pass from effort to achievement. *Is* the Charter a great landmark in history? Did it win liberties for the masses, for the "people of the towns and villages"? Is "the whole of the Constitutional History of England a commentary on this Charter"? Let us look at the Charter itself, and the demands of the barons, on which it was founded.

It is the fashion to put in the forefront of all accounts of these documents, their so-called "national" clauses, and to treat their "feudal" clauses (which can scarcely be ignored) as an unimportant tail-piece. That is hardly the way of the Charter itself; nor is it the plan which would naturally be followed by an impartial analyst. The Charter is usually divided into sixty-three clauses or articles. Of these, thirteen,[1] though important enough at the moment, are purely formal or temporary, and cannot possibly be "landmarks." They come at the end of the document, and their exclusion reduces the number of permanent clauses to fifty. Of these fifty clauses, *twenty-two*[2] are purely feudal, and they include twelve of the first sixteen articles of the Charter. Three[3] of the most famous of the remaining clauses concern "free men" only, about whom there will be a word to say. One clause (41) relates to merchants, one (13) to cities, two (1 and 22) guarantee clerical immunities. This leaves twenty-one[4] which may conceivably be of general application. We may summarize thus:

Formal and temporary clauses	13
Purely feudal	22
Free men	3
Merchants and cities	2
The Church	2
General	21
Total clauses in the Charter	63

But we are really making an extravagant allowance, if we admit that all, or even the bulk, of the twenty-one "general" clauses were of real importance to the common man of the thirteenth (or any other) century. To the peasant of John's reign, it would make little difference that the "inquest of life and limb" could be freely had without payment, that he might freely go forth of and return to the realm (he who rarely went beyond his own village during his whole life), that Common Pleas should not follow the King, that justices, sheriffs, and bailiffs should be learned in the law, that the writ of *Praecipe* should no longer be granted to the detriment of feudal claims, that the measure of London should be the standard of ale and barley. What did he care about these things? What the peasant of the thirteenth century desired, was, that he should not be tallaged at his lord's caprice, that his

[1] Nos. 49, 50, 51, 52, 53, 55, 56, 57, 58, 59, 61, 62, 63.
[2] 2, 3, 4, 5, 6, 7, 8, 9, 12, 14, 15, 16, 21, 26, 29, 31, 32, 34, 37, 43, 46, 47.
[3] 27, 30, 39.
[4] 10, 11, 17, 18, 19, 20, 23, 24, 25, 28, 33, 35, 36, 38, 40, 42, 44, 45, 48, 54, 60.

services should be fixed, that he should have a remedy for unjust eviction, that he might take his labour to another lord if he wished, that he might send his son to school, and marry his daughter without payment of a fine. There is no word in the Charter or the Articles to secure him these rights. The Londoners obtained the insertion in the Articles of a clause about borough tallage; but it did not appear in the Charter, its place being taken by a meaningless confirmation of "existing liberties and free customs."

But it is when we look at the Charter from the point of view of class distinction that we see how hollow is the claim of constitutional progress. The result of analysis is crushing. Six social classes are expressly mentioned by the Charter as recipients of rights, viz., earls and barons (among whom we may include the great ecclesiastics), knights, "free men" (*liberi homines*), clerics, merchants, villeins. Putting aside the "general" clauses, which may be assumed to benefit all alike, we may count up the number of rights accorded to each of these classes. Stated, for the sake of clearness, in tabular form, the figures are somewhat startling. We find that:

To the earls and barons are guaranteed	12 rights [5]
To the knights	11 " [6]
To the "free men"	4 " [7]
To the lower clergy is guaranteed	1 right [8]
To the merchants and burgesses are guaranteed	3 rights [9]
To the villeins is guaranteed	1 right [10]

[5] (1) Fixed "reliefs," (2) protection against abuses of guardianship, (3) fit marriages for infant heirs, (4) protection to widows, (5) protection of land from debts, (6) fixed aids and cutages, (7) fixed services, (8) assessment of fines by "peers," (9) freedom of taxation, (10) forfeitures of felon tenants' lands, (11) wardship of tenants' heirs, (12) custody of vacant abbeys which they have founded.

[6] All the above except (9) and (12), and, in addition, liberty to do castle guard in person, instead of paying money equivalent.

[7] (1) Moderate fines assessed by the "neighbourhood," (2) no seizure of goods on intestacy, (3) freedom from compulsory cartage, (4) trial by "peers."

[8] Freedom of benefices from fines.

[9] (1) Ancient liberties and customs, (2) moderate fines assessed by "neighbourhood," (3) freedom of trade.

[10] Moderate fines assessed by "neighbourhood."

This proportion is painfully suggestive of Falstaff's celebrated ratio between sack and bread.

We cannot, of course, get exact figures; but, according to Sir Henry Ellis' well-known estimate of the Domesday returns, the number of villeins was, in 1086, quite four-fifths of the whole population; and there is small reason to suppose that it was much less in 1215. In fact, few historians will care to dispute that, at the beginning of the thirteenth century, the vast majority of the dwellers in England were peasants, or that (to quote the high authority of Professor Vinogradoff) "the majority of the peasants are villeins." If to these we add the lower clergy, the merchants and the burgesses, we include all classes that can, by any fair use of the term, be called "popular"; and it would be a moderate estimate to reckon the total of these at five-sixths of the entire male population. If we were to reckon in the women and children dependent on them, we should, of course, get a higher proportion still. But what becomes of the "national" character of a document which guarantees *five* special rights to five-sixths of the so-called "nation," and *twenty-seven* to the remaining insignificant minority?

But here we touch what the writer firmly believes to be the great secret of the false glamour which invests Magna Carta. Three well-known clauses confer important rights upon the "free man" (*liber homo*); and a very natural confusion of ideas has created the belief, that this highly favoured person corresponds to the "simple freeman" of Teutonic legend, the "man in the street" of the modern Press. German scholars have even invented a special name for him—the *gemeinfrei,* or common freeman. Unhappily for this pleasing theory, the wording of the Charter itself renders it quite untenable. From that excellent source we learn certainly what the *liber homo* was not, and can shrewdly guess what he was. He was neither earl, baron, nor knight; but he certainly was not cleric, merchant, or villein, for the Charter draws, in three successive clauses,[11] an elaborate distinction between him and them.

As to what he was, it is not quite so clear. But he shared the aristocratic privilege of trial by "peers" (clause 39), he had a "contenement" (clause 20), and held a court (clause 34). Now, un-

11 20, 21, 22.

fortunately, we cannot be quite sure what a *contenementum* was, though no less a person than Selden, in after years, thought it meant the estate of a knight or baron. But we may be fairly sure, that the man who held a court, in the England of the thirteenth century, was more free than common. Strange things have been said of the English peasant of the later Middle Ages, but never yet that he rebelled against the King for interfering with his judicial dignity. In truth, the famous 39th clause, which protects the *liber homo* against seizure, imprisonment, disseisin, outlawry, exile, destruction, and attack by the King, was no magnificent declaration of the rights of the common man; it was simply a recognition of the privileges of an aristocratic class, a class of landowners, who, though not technically "feudal," can no more be ranked amongst "the people," than can the country gentleman of to-day.

(c) But the third, and, perhaps, the heaviest charge against the Charter is, that it was a positive stumbling block in the path of progress. Throughout it aims at consecrating that feudal organisation of society which, happily for the nation, was so soon to pass away. It has elsewhere been pointed out, by an accurate and cool-headed writer, that the rhetorical promises upon which its fame so largely rests were, for all practical purpose, valueless. It would be difficult to show how it secured the "freedom of the Anglican Church." To most observers it would seem, that that Church does not, even now, enjoy any very great measure of freedom—in the sense, at least, in which the word was understood in 1215. "To none will we sell, to none deny or delay, right or justice." It does not require much knowledge of the history of English Law to realise the hollowness of that promise. "It shall be lawful to every one to go forth of the realm" (except in time of war). But what about the writ *ne exeat regno*,[12] and the licence long required for travel? The famous "constitutional" clauses which are often referred to as guaranteeing the right of Parliamentary taxation, will not bear the test of reading for it is clear now (1) that they refer only to feudal burdens (2) that they contemplate a purely feudal assembly, and (3) that, happily for future progress, they disappeared from the Charter immediately after the death of John.[13]

12 'That he should not leave the realm'.
13 12, 14.

But it is not so generally realised, that some of the clauses of the Charter (and these not the least famous) are positively reactionary, and would, had they been observed have hampered seriously the progress of the next generation. By abolishing the writ of *Praecipe* (clause 34), the barons hoped to secure that darling treasure of feudal independence the monopoly of the manorial courts in suits concerning land. Happily, the clause was evaded, but only at the cost of cumbrous and costly fictions, which disgraced English legal procedure for six centuries. The claim to "trial by peers" was long supposed, by a curious freak of ignorance, to guarantee that "palladium of British liberties," trial by jury. As a matter of fact, it delayed indefinitely the adoption of that wholesome reform; and it is responsible, among other things, for the absurdities of the recent Russell case. The consecration of the lord's claim to the forfeiture of a felon's lands, for centuries worked a cruel injustice to the children of convicts, already, one would suppose, unfortunate enough; and many another oppressive feudal claim obtained a renewed lease of life from the clauses of the Charter. To suppose, in fact, that the barons who claimed the right, in the court of Philip Augustus, of disposing of the crown of England at their absolute discretion, were anxious to share their power with the people whom they plundered and taxed, is to make too great a demand on human credulity. The baronial leaders of 1215 had the inestimable advantage of fighting against a King who seemed determined, on every possible occasion, to put himself in the wrong; and they were not unwilling to strengthen their case by rhetorical flourishes about popular rights. But that they really intended to take the people into partnership, there is no scrap of evidence to show.

Finally, it is often triumphantly pointed out, that the Charter was re-issued no less than thirty-eight times, now on the mere volition of the royal advisers, now on the demand of reformers. The fact is admitted; but the inference appears strange. Why was it necessary to insist on the repeated confirmation of the Charter? Obviously, because it failed to do its work. At first it was firmly believed that this result was due to the violation of its provisions by the royal advisers. It was natural for an unlettered generation, mere children in the ways of political freedom, to take that view. But we, reading the long and stormy reign of John's son in the

light of later experience, can see that they were wrong. The
cunning favourites of Henry were very careful to observe the
letter of the law, just as were the unworthy ministers of Charles,
four centuries later. At last the truth began to dawn upon that
really national party, which the evils of Henry's reign slowly
brought into existence. The demand for the Charter is still raised;
but chiefly as an ancient and stirring battle cry. It is perceived
that the Charter is not enough. It consecrates the past, not the
future. It leaves the King in full possession of his feudal claim to
exact tallage, it leaves him free to invent new taxes, it makes no
provision for national representation, it allows the ministers of
state to be selected purely by royal caprice. The entire break with
the past attempted by the Reformers at the Parliament of Oxford
in 1258, shows that at last this truth was realised; and, from that
time, the demand for the Charter becomes a matter of form. The
scheme of 1258 was too revolutionary; it succeeded only for a
moment. But, in the long reign of Edward I, the compromise
between King and people was slowly worked out, until, at its
end, our scheme of government assumed the shape which it preserved, save for brief intervals, till the Revolution of 1688. But it
was not the Charter which brought about this result. All the
happy changes which we associate with the name of Edward—the
creation of a national Parliament, the renunciation of the irregular taxes, free trade in land, the perpetual peace of the King, the
right of the subject to remedy against the royal officials, the con-
cordat between Church and State, the organisation of the coast
guard, the reform of the Exchequer—all these were the work of
men who were unborn, or in their cradles, when the Charter was
signed at Runnymede. And the very vice, not of the Charter
itself, but of the literary adulation which in later years grew up
around it, is, that it turns the eyes of the Englishman away from
a period full of real interest and abundant suggestion, to fix them
upon a melodramatic and somewhat tawdry scene in a turgid and
unwholesome drama. John, and William Marshal, and even
Stephen Langton, are not to be mentioned in the same breath
with Edward, and Robert Burnell, and Winchelsey. The scene
before Westminster Hall, on the 14th July, 1297, when the great
King, thwarted in his skilful plans by the selfish quibbles of his
barons, cast himself passionately upon the support of his people,
and received from them equally passionate expressions of their

trust and love, is a far nobler subject for a national poet or painter, than the hollow truce at Runnymede, when a conspiracy of self-seeking and reckless barons wrung from a worthless monarch the concession of feudal privileges, which he never for one moment intended to observe.

In truth it does not require much historical knowledge to discover the real author of the Myth of Magna Carta. He was a man whose lot was cast in troublous times, amid the angry mutterings of that coming struggle which was to light the torch of civil war in England. Deeply pledged to the popular side in that struggle, he cast into it all the weight of his profound if somewhat undigested learning, and his powerful if somewhat unscrupulous intellect. It was an age in which historical discoveries were received with credulity, in which the canons of historical criticism were yet unformulated. Doubtless, more than one of Coke's contemporaries (John Selden, for example) must have had a fairly shrewd idea that Coke was mingling his politics with his historical research. But, for the most part, those competent to criticise Coke's research were of his way of thinking in politics, and did not feel called upon to quarrel with their own supporter. Zeal for historical truth is apt to pale before the fiercer flame of zeal for political victory. It is a tribute to Coke's character and ability, that he imposed his ingenious but unsound historical doctrines, not only on an uncritical age, but on succeeding ages which deem themselves critical. It is not, perhaps, altogether a testimony to the industry and acumen of a generation which might well be impartial in such matters, that the legend invented by Coke has been so long allowed to pass current as the gospel of history.

9 FROM   *J. C. Holt*
          Rights and Liberties in Magna Carta, 1960

*The conflict between the views of Stubbs and Jenks has been
circumvented rather than resolved. Attention has come to be con-
centrated on relating the charter to the contemporary circumstances which produced it and determined its tone and content.
Even so some modern studies, especially those concerned with the
form and language in which the argument between King John
and his opponents was cast, are very relevant to the debate.
The following paper, the whole of which is reproduced here, examines the two critical concepts of "rights" and "liberties" in
their contemporary setting.*

___

In 1236 John the Scot, earl of Chester, was summoned before
King Henry III to answer charges that he had deprived certain
heirs of their rightful inheritance. In his objections to the charge
the Earl finally alleged that as this was a common plea it should
be held in a definite place and not before the King; the procedure
was therefore contrary "to the liberties and charter granted by the
Lord King." He was referring of course, to Magna Carta. This
kind of appeal to the terms of the Great Charter was frequently
made both in important legal actions and in political crises in the
course of the thirteenth century. The document had a practical
value and, as Miss Faith Thompson has shown, this contributed
in no small measure to its survival as a factor in English history.
    This, however, is not the whole story. Lawyers, historians and
politicians have for centuries seen the Charter not just as a collection of practical regulations but as a statement of principles. Individual liberty, trial by jury, freedom of trade, the supremacy of
the law, the separation of justice from politics, all these ideas and
others have been read in, and sometimes into, it. We may reason-

SOURCE. *Album Helen Maud Cam*, vol. 1 (Studies presented to the Inter-
national Commission for the History of Representative and Parliamentary
Institutions, XXIII, Louvain, 1960), pp. 57–69. Reprinted by permission of
Nauwelaerts Edition and Miss Marjorie Cam.

ably ask whether this is justified. The original charter was a very uncertain political compromise, unacceptable to many of the parties involved and legally valid for only a few months in the summer of 1215. How did this document come to dominate English history as it has done? Was it simply a result of the way in which re-issues and confirmations were piled one upon the other, buttressed by appeals, interpretations and misinterpretations? Or was there in addition, at the start, some kind of Promethean act? If so, wherein, for contemporaries, lay its creative quality?

The bull of August 24, 1215, whereby Pope Innocent annulled the first charter did not kill it stone dead. Despite the fact that the 1225 version was the only one binding in law, the 1215 charter was still being transcribed faithfully into legal collections at the end of the thirteenth century. The apparently clumsy errors made by Roger of Wendover and Matthew Paris in entering the Charter into their chronicles show that some men failed to distinguish between the various re-issues even to the extent of imagining that the Charter of the Forest of 1217 was first made at Runnymede two years earlier. To contemporaries then, the prime source was the 1215 document: to it Wendover in the late 1220's and Paris thirty years later traced an unbroken line of political ideas and administrative practices. This continuity was not a fancy of the St. Albans writers but was there in fact. Ten out of the Twenty Five guarantors of 1215 were numbered among the witnesses to the charter of 1225.

This interest in the 1215 document could yield no practical value in the courts of law. We may even doubt whether there would have been such frequent appeal to the 1225 document if to contemporaries it had constituted a set of rules and regulations and nothing more. One hundred and twenty five years earlier King Henry I had issued a coronation charter which defined procedure on several important issues in feudal practice and other matters. But while, as we have seen, John, earl of Chester, was quick to appeal to Magna Carta in 1236, his great-grandfather Ranulf Gernons, earl of Chester, that great tormentor of King Stephen, showed no interest, as far as we know, in the charter of Henry I; nor did any of the other turbulent figures of his period. Henry's charter indeed never enjoyed such constitutional signifi-

cance as Magna Carta achieved, until it became a cardinal point
in the baronial attack on John and was hence involved in the
genesis of the Great Charter itself. Clearly, for the survival of such
a document as a political force, practical concessions, even several
of them, were not enough. We may accept that the political situation after 1215 was different from that after 1100 in many ways,
and that English society and government had changed in the
century or so between the two documents. But behind all this
there is the simple stark fact that Henry's charter, as far as we
know, aroused little feeling at the time. Magna Carta, in contrast,
set light to passions and ideas which burned immediately, fiercely
and permanently. It is with this in mind that I intend to examine
what Magna Carta and certain closely associated documents have
to say about "rights" and "liberties."

The Great Charter in the first place uses these words in a quite
common, traditional sense. Rights and liberties are those things
to which we are entitled by law. Of the two, "rights" is perhaps
the wider term, for "rights" may be enjoyed by custom whereas
"liberties" are more usually privileges to which we are entitled by
royal grant or prescription. But the terms were close enough to
each other to be frequently associated, as, for example, when the
corroboration clause of the Charter refers to the "liberties, rights
and concessions" which it contains. Rights and liberties might be
incorporeal but they were not abstract. Men could petition for
them, sue for them and be sued for them. They had a value which
could be assessed. In this sense, if not tangible in themselves, the
profits they yielded were usually so. Cap. 52 of the 1215 Charter,
which provided for the restitution of rights and liberties of which
individuals had been unlawfully deprived, and the various writs
in the Close Rolls executing this clause, make perfectly clear what
might be comprehended under these terms. One man recovers a
castle, another land, another the right to hold a market and fair,
another the liberty whereby his dogs could run freely within the
royal forest of Northumberland. Some recover "liberties" in the
more specific sense of jurisdictional franchises. All this would
have been readily comprehended two or three generations earlier.
We are faced with a traditional use of words and with traditional
ideas, part and parcel of the everyday assumptions men made
about the feudal society in which they lived, part and parcel too

of those concepts of hierarchy and status which stemmed back to the Investiture Controversy and far beyond.

These simple usages which we find in the Charter were not the only ones in force in the early thirteenth century. The influence of canon and Roman law in the course of the twelfth century had had here a marked and important effect. Thus the terms *ius* and *iura* came to be used not only in the sense of right or title but also in the sense of law. This is clearly marked in the work of Glanville where the word is used in both senses; he not only talks of the right of an heir or the right to an advowson[1] but also of the *ius et consuetudo regni* (the law and custom of the realm) and the *iura regni* (the laws of the realm). To him the *ius* or *iura regni* constituted a body of substantive law, something which might be associated with the custom of the realm, but something which was stronger than custom, something which might be compared with the canons of the Church and the Roman law of the *Corpus Iuris Civilis*.

The distinction between these two senses of the word *ius* or *iura* is easily grasped and was easily grasped in the twelfth century. The most cursory glance at Justinian's Institutes would make the difference in usage clear. But confusion might and did in fact occur. The most obvious example of this is the Great Charter itself. It is in fact a grant of rights and liberties, but it became a body of law, the first item in the Statute Book, and, as Maitland put it, "the nearest approach to an irrepealable fundamental statute that England has ever had." Its unique character arose partly from this confusion. Unlike a normal grant of liberties the grantee was not a precisely named individual or institution, nor was there a clearly established procedure of suit or doctrine of seisin and ownership which might be used to reinforce and protect the original grant. Unlike the custom of the land, the Charter as law was an obvious artefact, worse still an artefact about which men had argued and fought. It therefore lacked in many of its sections the long usage then considered so essential to substantive law. It was something new in its principles even more than in its provisions. It was no accident that it required such frequent confirmation in the years which followed.

[1] Magna Carta 1215, cap. 17.

The reasons for this confusion and the way it had developed provide an important clue in understanding the Great Charter and the rôle it came to play in the thirteenth century. There were many different, sometimes conflicting, influences at work on English legal thinking and Englishmen's assumptions about government. There were the normal feudal notions of the king's responsibilities towards his vassals and of the exercise of government by their advice. There were older ideas of law as an expression of the will of a community. Roman influences were pointing, very hesitantly and uncertainly, towards a concept of kingship as a legally supreme public authority. While early twelfth century legal collections treat royal power as personal and speak simply of the rights of the King, at the beginning of the next century men will talk of the rights of the Crown. But if these ideas were giving emphasis to royal authority, an equally powerful train of thought stemming from the Church was teaching that kingship was office and that a king carried heavy responsibilities. In 1215 itself, Archbishop Stephen Langton was a powerful influence behind such views with the emphasis he laid upon John's coronation oath.

The effects of these cross-currents are most clearly seen in the work of the well known anonymous writer, perhaps a Londoner, who produced a new edition of the Laws of Edward the Confessor[2] at the beginning of the thirteenth century. The additions which he made to the traditional text clearly illustrate the dilemma of his period. There is hint of it in the title he gives this section for he is concerned on the one hand with the rights of the Crown, and on the other with the office of the King. We then read "The King ought by right, to preserve and defend completely, in their integrity and without delapidation, all lands and honours, all dignities and rights and liberties of the Crown of this kingdom, and restore with all his power to their due and former state the *iura regni* which have been dispersed, destroyed or lost". By the side of this he can state that the king is the Vicar of God who has the duty to protect and defend the people of God and Holy Church, and within a few lines he is busy subjecting him very strictly to the advice of the magnates of the realm and prescribing that he should rule according to the law. Clearly we cannot look

2 The Laws of Edward the Confessor, a law-book compiled c. 1130, which seeks to amalgamate Old English law with twelfth-century procedure.

here for the logic of an expert in political theory. Nor should we seek it either now or later. Bracton's[3] difficulties on the relationship of the king to law are well known. King John, when the situation required conciliatory language, would express his personal concern at complaints directed against his sheriffs. Henry III, in similar circumstances, would emphasize his regard for the "common interest of the whole kingdom," and that celebrated martinet in the matter of baronial franchises, Edward I, would on other matters happily exploit the Roman-law tag 'what touches all should be approved by all.'

Nevertheless political views need not be logical to be influential or dangerous or even successful. At the heart of this idea of the rights of the Crown there was an essential vagueness similar to that I have already noted in the Great Charter itself. Among these rights of the Crown was the exercise of justice. The concept of the rights of the crown quickly passes into Glanville's concept of the laws of the kingdom. The rights of the Crown are not just rights, they are also responsibilities to which the King is bound not just in his own interest but by virtue of his office. The different possibilities here were laid bare in 1215 and 1216. Innocent III denounced the Charter as decreasing and impairing John's royal rights and dignity to the detriment of the royal right and the shame of the English nation. Prince Louis of France in contrast could condemn King John for failing to preserve the "rights and customs of the church and realm of England." Once in this last position we are passing from the rights of the Crown, through the idea of the *iura regni* as the laws of the realm to the idea of *iura regni* as the rights of the kingdom. This last was the crucial step in the attack on the government of the Angevin monarchs.

This step was taken very early in the barons' campaign against the government. As early as 1205, according to Gervase of Canterbury, they compelled the King to swear that he would preserve the *iura regni* by their advice. By 1213 they were coming to identify their own liberties and rights with the liberties and rights of the kingdom for which warrant might be found in customary law and especially in the laws of St. Edward and Henry I. The Coggeshall chronicler thus sees the Northern barons in 1214 as work-

[3] Henry of Bracton, royal justice 1245 to 1268 when he died. Author of *The Laws and Customs of England*, the fundamental work on the law of medieval England.

ing to force the king to reform the liberties of the church and the
kingdom and to abolish evil customs. This transference from
baronial liberties to the liberties of the realm, from ancient rights
to ancient laws, was much facilitated by the baronial exploitation
of the Charter of Henry I, a document which like the Great
Charter itself, partook of the character both of a grant of privileges and of a legal enactment.

The Great Charter itself will have none of this. Here we see
all the passions and prejudices and propaganda of the quarrel
through a glass skillfully darkened by chancery clerks who were
concerned to produce a document in which there should be no
avoidable diminution of the King's majesty and which should
come as close as possible to the normal diplomatic forms. The
equation of baronial liberties with the laws and liberties of the
kingdom is something they cannot stomach. They will not accept
the opposition claim to act for the realm. Hence the liberties in
the Charter are not granted to the realm or to a community. Well
established institutions they will accept. Thus the city of London
is to have all its ancient liberties and customs under cap. 13 and
cap. 1 states that the English church shall be free and shall hold
its rights and liberties unharmed. Less fortunate mortals outside
these corporate bodies, however, are only permitted to enjoy their
newly won grant severally. The liberties of the Charter are
granted not to the kingdom but to the freemen of the kingdom.
This form is used consistently throughout the whole document.
Only in cap. 61 where there is a reference to the commune of the
whole land, is there the slightest hint that all free men might
constitute a community or a realm, and this perhaps represents
ideas emanating from London rather than from the main line of
the baronial argument.

At this point the Great Charter clearly plays into the hands of
those later critics who have seen in it a grant of privileges or liberties and nothing more. But the interpretation which the chancery
clerks placed on the document can and should be questioned.
Many of its clauses, naturally enough, place no difficulty in the
way of this interpretation. The regulations about baronial reliefs
in cap. 2 represent concessions which every tenant-in-chief of the
Crown can hold as an individual. Widows and minors likewise,
can hold severally the concessions made in their interest. But who
is to hold the concession in cap. 40 that right and justice shall

not be sold, denied or delayed? And, if the cynic insists on dismissing this clause as windy piety, who is to hold the concession of cap. 45 that only those who know the law of the land and are willing to observe it shall be employed as justices, constables, sheriffs and bailiffs? Who again is to hold the concession that shires, hundreds, wapentakes and tithings must be held at the ancient farms, or the concession of the charter of 1217 regulating the sheriff's tourns? Clearly in these instances, whatever Magna Carta says about itself, we are faced with rights which, if they are to mean anything, must be held not severally but in common, by a community, whether that community be hundred, shire or kingdom.

If the men who drafted the Great Charter would not recognize this, others would. The Dunstable Annalist, an almost contemporary authority, refers to the "Charters concerning the liberties of the realm of England." Documents closely associated with the Charter, some drawn up in greater haste, others originating outside the Chancery, also show fewer inhibitions in accepting the baronial arguments and assumptions. Thus cap. 48 of the Articles of the Barons bluntly states that the king has conceded customs and liberties to the kingdom. More strikingly still the treaty concerning the temporary custody of London was drawn up between the King on the one hand, and on the other, the baronial leaders, who were named, and "other earls barons and free men of the whole kingdom." It goes on to refer to the "Charter concerning the liberties and security granted to the kingdom." The attitude represented in these words was perhaps best summed up three months after Runnymede, when three of the baronial leaders, in letters addressed to one of the king's agents, Brian de Lisle, referred to the "charter to the commune of the realm."

In recent years there has been some trenchant and justified criticism of the way in which Stubbs used the concept of the nation. Whatever may be said of other instances, these phrases I have cited clearly give him some warrant for using this concept in the case of Magna Carta. Some contemporaries, if they did not believe that the Charter belonged to the nation with all the nineteenth century assumptions which Stubbs might attach to that word, at least believed that it belonged to the kingdom. They were not, of course, attempting to argue that there were two separate powers, king and realm, related to each other by covenant. The

Charter is not, and was not imagined as, a social contract. But they were claiming that the good of the realm was not simply a matter for the King and his immediate advisers, that if the Crown could claim rights then the kingdom as a whole could claim rights and that, in this situation, baronial opinion was not just representative of the baronage or even of other groups as well, but was representative of the whole community, of the whole realm. Within a few years Roger of Wendover will put into the mouth of yet another notable recalcitrant baron, Earl Richard Marshal, these words: "the King is not as powerful as God and God is justice itself. In Him I place my trust in seeking and preserving my own and the kingdom's right." Wendover's great successor, Matthew Paris, will later casually note on the death of Warin de Monchensy, a baron whose chief distinction lay apparently in his great wealth, that he was "a zealous supporter of the peace and liberty of the realm."

The crux of the baronial argument lay in the construction they were placing on one single word, "realm." This, in their view denoted a social group, a community, which could be possessed of both rights and functions. The King was a part of this, certainly, but a part whose relationship to the whole could be prescribed and was now in fact being prescribed by a process of royal grant or kingly self-limitation. The royal interpretation of the word, as expressed by the chancery clerks in the early versions of the Charter, was quite different. Here the realm is a royal possession, that area which the rule of their master, as king, pervades. The liberties of the charter are to be held "by all men of our realm within our realm of England."[4] To the king the realm is always "*our* realm," an assumption against which the rebels of 1215 now set an increasingly damaging question mark.

In Magna Carta we are dealing with the origins of the concept of the community of the realm. It is the first great expression of the will of that community, and thereafter its rallying cry. But care is needed. The "community of the realm" has never been, and can never be. Interests conflict; some men govern others. The community of the realm exists not in fact but in the arguments and minds of men. What the barons claim in 1215 the knights and bachelors will claim in 1259 and the peasantry in 1381. Too

4 Cap. 25.

much has perhaps been made of the fact that the Charter of 1215 was granted not to the baronage but to the freemen of the kingdom, that it was concerned with legal procedures which were enjoyed by all freemen, and that it contained concessions to townsfolk and those concerned in trade. English law recognized few distinctions between the great tenants-in-chief of the King and the free tenants at large. Throughout the 12th century and particularly in the latter half, both groups had been associated more closely and often in interchangeable rôles in the work of government. There were barons who were comparatively poor and insignificant. There were men of simple knightly rank who were wealthy and held sway over the minds of kings and the lives of men. Most barons engaged in trade, sometimes directly, more usually through factors. Some barons were also burgesses. Some burgesses, in contrast, became knights and occasionally barons. Some burgesses were treated as barons. All this points to the rashness of thinking that any particular group of clauses in the Charter illustrates a high minded baronial concern for the interests of other sections of the population, for these interests and their own could not be separated. Such thinking acquires an additionally reckless air when we remember that the protagonists of the Charter were concerned with acquiring political support in a very critical situation. In 1215, as at many other times, knights and burgesses, and barons too, could be bought.

But if we are playing in some newly sprung and potent fount of self-deception, it derived from waters deep and plentiful. The close-knit society of the English shires, the *patria,* the county; the remarkable cohesion of the King's government; that England was "fortunate in littleness and insularity," as Maitland put it; that she had come under the hand of William the Conqueror by conquest and yet by a very peculiar conquest; these and many other influences combined to give a real background to the idea of the community of the realm. It was derived from social facts. If we reject the picture of the baronage as high minded idealists it must not be to paint another of them as logic-chopping and argumentative dons. We may see too many principles where in fact there were only the subtleties of political debate. In cap. 12 of the 1215 charter, for example, King John's opponents were not concerned with the principle of national consent to taxation, nor even with the practice of baronial consent to feudal aids, for neither John

nor his predecessors had needed to attack this; they were simply
trying to use the established procedure on aids to create a quite
novel and revolutionary procedure in the matter of scutage. Here
we are faced with muddled thinking, but muddled thinking to a
very material and immediate purpose.

This concern for immediate mundane matters was never far
distant. In a famous legal action in 1226 a group of Lincolnshire
knights and gentry chose to attack the sheriff's administration of
justice in the courts of Lincolnshire and Kesteven.[5] Their case
was a simple one, namely that he had exceeded his duties as laid
down by custom and chapter 35 of the 1217 charter. Led by two
knights, Theobald Hautein and Hugh of Humby, they argued
that the sheriff had behaved "contrary to their liberty which they
ought to hold by the charter of the Lord King." "As they held
these liberties from the Lord King, it seemed to them that the
position of the shire court could not and ought not to be changed
except with the Lord King and the magnates of the realm." Here
an appeal to the Charter takes us straight from local privilege and
practices to the concept of the king and magnates as the guardians
of the law, into ideas typical of the political debates of the thirteenth century. This case was typical of its time, too, in that in
1234 the King and barons came to decide on some of the points
which had been raised and drew up an ordinance which clarified
cap. 35 of the 1217 charter. It was also later extracted by Bracton
into his Note Book. Knights, barons, a famous king's justice and
the King himself all had an interest in it. But what were Theobald Hautein and his fellows concerned with immediately? They
had spent one day at the shire court hearing pleas, so they alleged,
from dawn to dusk. They did not want to be troubled by a second
day's hard work. The shire court must last for the customary
single day and no more. When the sheriff attempted to transfer
the outstanding cases to the next meeting of the wapentakes of
Kesteven they were even unwilling to allow him this short cut.
They saw themselves vexed with exactions and injuries. It was as
simple as that. The Charter was thus a very material defence of
custom and privilege of a very material kind. It was long to
remain so. A volume dealing with Sherwood forest in Notting-

[5] Lincolnshire comprised the three subdivisions of Lindsey, Kesteven and
the Parts of Holland.

hamshire, written early in the fifteenth century, is prefaced with the following note: *Memorandum,* the Charter of the Forest is under patent in the hands and custody of Lord Ralph Cromwell Junior, and the Charter of Liberties is under patent in the hands and custody of Nicholas of Strelley, and the perambulation of the forest of Sherwood made in the time of Henry III is under patent in the hands of William Jorce or Burton. Like good lawyers, the landowners of Nottinghamshire were still keeping the essential works of reference at their elbow.

10   FROM   *J. C. Holt*
      Magna Carta: Law and Constitution, 1965

The following paper, which is reproduced in full, investigates the links between the fact and the myth of Magna Carta. It was originally a radio broadcast given on the occasion of the 750th Anniversary of Magna Carta for the British Broadcasting Corporation.

The continued veneration of Magna Carta is one of the more mysterious impulses of the British body politic. It is an old document concerned with political and social institutions very different from our own. It was not unique in its own time. Similar grants of liberties were made in other European countries in the thirteenth and fourteenth centuries, in France, Germany, Hungary, and Aragon. None of these has shown the same power of survival: Frenchmen commemorate the fall of the Bastille, not the charters of liberties which Louis X granted to them in 1315. The continued vigour of Magna Carta is all the more remarkable in that those most closely concerned with it have not been unduly enthusiastic. Lawyers have concurred in the repeal of chap-

SOURCE. J. C. Holt, "Magna Carta: law and constitution," *The Listener,* vol. 74, no. 1893, July 8, 1965, pp. 47–9.

ter after chapter. Historians have been critical. Yet the charter
has survived both repeal and criticism.

Some aspects of this long history are easily explicable. Magna
Carta survived because its original sense was distorted. Its most
famous chapter, cap. 39, originally laid down that lawful process
should precede execution. In the fourteenth century, this provision, originally a privilege conveyed to free men, was extended
by statutory confirmation to all men of "whatsoever estate or
condition" they might be. The "lawful judgment of peers" of
the original charter was now equated with trial by jury and the
"law of the land" of the original with due process of law. This
was only the beginning. In the seventeenth century the parliamentary and legal opposition to the Stuart kings revived these
fourteenth-century interpretations and then went on to associate
this chapter with the procedure of *habeas corpus*. Sir Edward
Coke even argued that a man's property included his right to buy
and sell; hence, he maintained, Magna Carta was contravened
by grants of patents of monopoly. Even this was not the end.
Coke's view of the Charter was exported and absorbed across the
Atlantic, where due process of law was ultimately built into
the Fifth and Fourteenth Amendments of the Constitution of the
United States, to continue a long history as a defence of individual liberty and economic *laissez-faire*. Other sections of the charter underwent similar changing interpretations. Thus there
emerged a potent myth that the charter was a statement of individual liberty which governments infringed at their peril.

The charter was also exalted as some kind of ancient and fundamental law, which stood in a debatable relationship to parliamentary sovereignty, but which the royal prerogative could not
touch. Indeed the existence and nature of the charter does much
to explain that strong current of antiquarian thought which
dominated political argument in the seventeenth century until
the advent of Hobbes and Locke. It is not simply that the charter was already venerable. Coke and others argued not merely
that it was ancient law, but that it embodied a law already ancient at the time of the charter's promulgation. And for this the
charter itself was responsible. It did in fact assert and imply that
it was a statement of ancient custom. The barons who won it had
appealed for the restoration of their ancient liberties, demanded
the revival of the laws of Edward the Confessor and Henry I, and

sought the confirmation of Henry's coronation charter. Already under John men contrasted Norman tyranny with the good and ancient custom of Anglo-Saxon England. "You are not worthy to be compared to St. Edward," cried the papal nuncio Pandulf to King John, "you relish and enforce the evil laws of William the Bastard, and you despise the best laws of St. Edward as if they were worthless." The barons' arguments in 1215 were not uncontested. They claimed that they were reviving ancient liberties, but the agents of Pope Innocent III condemned them for introducing new laws. Truth lay on both sides. Ancient authority was just as specious, and just as hotly debated as in 1640.

This method of political argument became more complicated as time passed as it was reinforced by the concept and practice of judicial interpretation, by the antiquarian revival which followed the dissolution of the monasteries and the consequent dispersal of manuscripts, and by the Puritan emphasis on the scriptures. But the source was Magna Carta. The usual charge against Coke, that he distorted the original meaning of the charter, thus seems unreal, for what he distorted was already a distortion. The original charter was not some kind of datum from which all subsequent departure was unjustifiable. Moreover, the process of distortion, if we are to call it that, was much more gradual than much of the criticism of Coke would allow. It was not so much distortion as interpretation and development. Those very words of chapter 39, "lawful judgment of peers" and "the law of the land," on which later generations were to exercise their interpretative talents, were very far from clear when they were first enunciated. Indeed they were already under dispute within twenty years of 1215. "There are no peers in England," claimed King Henry III's minister, Peter des Roches, in 1233.

Magna Carta was simply a stage in a long and discontinuous debate about the relationship between law and sovereign authority. How important a stage? The charter embodied and elucidated the principle that government is subject to law. But it was not alone in doing this. Even King John accepted the assumption that a king, unlike a tyrant, ruled according to law. Indeed, he and his predecessors had helped to create some of the law which Magna Carta aimed to preserve. The charter helped to establish the idea of the community of the realm. It was granted to all the free men of the realm, and it assumed that the privileges which

it conveyed would be held by the community. But here it summed
up trends which, in the acquisition of liberties by towns, shires,
and other local groups, had been under way for nearly a century.
The charter was produced in a feudal society dominated politi-
cally by a small number of territorial magnates. This need detract from the principles it embodied no more than the social
structure of fourth-century B.C. Athens invalidates the work of
Aristotle. In short, it can be left to stand as a statement of legal
and political principles.

But if we permit this, it is advisable to note the obvious pit-
falls in such an approach. If at its best it gives recognition to the
continuous element in English political thinking, at its worst it
represents Whig history and the anachronistic imposition of the
present on the past. Moreover, it is only too easy to assume that
the men at Runnymede in 1215 were visited by some kind of
plenary inspiration which enabled them to speak forth constitutional wisdom hitherto unplumbed. Of this there is no evidence.
Indeed, few men made very much of the charter at the time. It
was called great not because of its quality, as Coke thought, but
because of its size and in order to distinguish the 1217 and subsequent reissues from the companion Charter of the Forest. Some
contemporary writers who described the war between King John
and his barons did not bother to mention it. Some quoted or
summarized it, not always accurately. Only one gave it in full
and he bungled the text. The original version was annulled by
Pope Innocent III on August 24, 1215. Its terms were never properly enforced. It was the reissue of 1217, subsequently confirmed
in 1225, which became part of the law of the land. Even this
amended version owed its birth to the fact that Henry III was a
boy of nine when he came to the throne. This was an inauspicious
beginning for a document from which so much has stemmed.

The later history of Magna Carta seems all the more remarkable when set against a wider context. A hundred and fifteen
years earlier Henry I had issued a coronation charter. It contained important privileges, some of which were repeated or extended in Magna Carta. Yet nothing happened. Henry I's grant
was a dead letter until it became involved in the genesis of the
Great Charter itself. Similarly there was no later rival to Magna
Carta for centuries to come. Its prestige was scarcely matched
until the Petition of Right of 1628 and the Bill of Rights of

1689. Even then, Pitt still associated Magna Carta with these two as the bible of the English constitution. The reasons for this prominence are not accidental. They are not to be found in the history of the "myth" of Magna Carta in later centuries. They lie in the nature of the charter itself and in the situation in and immediately after 1215.

In all except form the charter was the first example of what later generations were to call statute. It did not achieve this status immediately, but statute is what the charter became in effect within a generation of 1215. It was not enrolled until 1297, but that it was the prototype of later legislation is demonstrated by the fact that it figured almost inevitably in manuscript collections of statutes in the thirteenth century, along with the Statute or Provisions of Merton of 1236 and the legislation of Edward I.

Needless to say, men did not consciously create statute in making Magna Carta. They were simply trying to meet the difficulties of their circumstances. They sought concessions which limited the power of the Crown. Yet they could find no more effective instrument for such concessions than a solemn grant under the royal seal. There was no other instrument available. They took every possible care in 1215 to try to ensure that the charter gave no hint at all that it had been achieved through rebellion. And they took unavailing precautions to try to exclude papal intervention and annulment.

The charter also firmly asserted that it was a concession made in perpetuity. "We have also granted," it ran, "to all the free men of our realm for ourselves and our heirs for ever, all the liberties written below, to have and to hold, them and their heirs from us and our heirs." Yet they knew very well that perpetuity was a vague concept, and that equally solemn grants, allegedly made in perpetuity, did in fact require frequent confirmation, for example at the accession of a new king. Hence they were extremely sensitive to any hint that the Great Charter and the companion Charter of the Forest might be rescinded. When in 1224 one of King John's old supporters, William Briwerre, advised the young King Henry that the charters were invalid because they had been exacted by force, he was silenced by the Archbishop, Stephen Langton, who warned him not to disturb the peace of the realm. There was still some doubt even after 1225 when the charters reached their final form, for although this version emphasized that King Henry granted them freely in return for a subsidy, nevertheless the king was still a minor and hence was incapable of making grants in perpetuity. When he achieved his majority in 1227 there were rumours that he intended to rescind the charters and it was not in fact until 1237, twenty-two years after Runnymede, when Henry issued a charter of confirmation, that they finally achieved completely unimpeachable validity. By then, indeed, they had been given a very special position. The reissues of 1225 and 1237 were reinforced by sentence of excommunication against any who infringed them. This was renewed at the next formal confirmation in 1253 and repeatedly thereafter. The charters thus enjoyed a more than secular authority.

Within a generation or so, then, Magna Carta achieved some kind of permanence; the perpetuity envisaged in 1215 was made to mean something. Here another feature of the charter was important. It was not simply a grant of privileges which the Crown could acknowledge and then wash its hands of. It was also law, which had to be enforced and perhaps adjusted and developed. For this lawyers—or at least judges and administrators of the law —were largely responsible. Their influence on the charters increased with each successive document. It is more marked in the Magna Carta of 1215 than in the preliminary terms which preceded it, the so-called Articles of the Barons; the charter is precisely and comprehensively phrased where the Articles are vaguer and less provident. It is more marked again in the reissue of 1216, which contained a number of precisely conceived amendments, even though it was hastily produced as a bid for support in the middle of a civil war. It is emphatic in the charter of 1217 into which completely new regulations were inserted on the management of local courts and on alienation of land held by feudal service. Lawyers used Magna Carta just as their successors under Edward I used statute. The next statute, the Provisions of Merton of 1236, demonstrates the intervening stage between the charter and the Edwardian legislation. It was concerned in half its provisions with the further elucidation of matters contained in the charter of 1217. Like the charter of 1215, it was produced after a discussion of articles. It was not yet completely free from the language of a grant. King and council still provided and conceded; they did not yet establish and ordain.

Magna Carta, then, stands at the source of English statute law. There is an important corollary. Closely associated with the later myth of Magna Carta there was another idea, that the law of England protected rather than restricted the individual's liberty and freedom. This was not unchallenged; the law, even Magna Carta, had its critics among the radicals in the modern period and among the peasantry in the medieval. There were those, like the Leveller, Richard Overton, who thought the charter "but a beggarly thing containing many marks of intolerable bondage." But the equation of law and liberty was generally accepted with little question. Overton himself went to gaol with Coke's Commentary on Magna Carta[1] clasped to his bosom.

Already in the fifteenth century, Sir John Fortescue, Chief Justice of the King's Bench of Henry VI, could enumerate the Englishman's blessings as follows:

"They are not brought to trial except before the ordinary judges, where they are treated justly according to the law of the land. Nor are they examined or impleaded in respect of their chattels, or possessions, nor arrested for crime of whatever magnitude and enormity, except according to the laws of that land and before the aforesaid judges."

Here he was praising English law to the disadvantage of the civil law of France. He was also calling on a theme which went back to the early history of the Great Charter, for it was then that liberties and law were first confused. When barons and knights insisted that liberties should be law and lawyers added law to liberties they not only invented statute, but also created one of the most venerated and treasured articles of faith of English political life.

[1] *The Second Part of Institutes,* on which see no. 12(d).

PART TWO

The Survival of Magna Carta

CONFIRMATIONS AND ENFORCEMENT

11 FROM   *Faith Thompson*
        The First Century of Magna Carta, 1925

Magna Carta persisted as a document for two reasons:

1. Its confirmation was sought repeatedly in the recurrent po litical crises of the thirteenth century. The first reissues of 1216 and 1217 were part of the settlement of civil war which had begun in 1215. The definitive text of 1225 preceded Henry III's majority. Thereafter the most important confirmations occurred in 1237, 1253, 1265, 1297, and 1300. By 1301 the charter and the Charter of the Forest had been reissued or confirmed on at least fifteen occasions.

2. Particular chapters of the charter were enforced in the courts of law. Increasingly it was subjected to judicial and later parliamentary interpretation.

Professor Faith Thompson, who made the later history of Magna Carta her life's work, here examines an aspect of the first process: the arrangement for the publication and enforcement of the charter in the thirteenth century.

SOURCE. Faith Thompson, *The First Century of Magna Carta*, Research Publications of the University of Minnesota, Studies in the Social Sciences, no. 16, 1925, pp. 93–104. Reprinted by permission of University of Minnesota Press.

PUBLICATION

The extent to which the Great Charter was known, in name at least, must have been increased by the dramatic events of its origin: the scene at Runnymede where the "liberties" were forced from a reluctant sovereign; the annulling of the Charter by the pope; the recourse to civil war to maintain the liberties, even to the calling in of the French prince and his army; finally the death of the tyrant and defeat of the invader; the crowning of the boy king, and the reissue of the liberties in a revised Charter, sanctioned by the pope, sealed by his legate, and protected by the anathemas of the church. It all made a good story, one which lost nothing in the telling as time went on. The fact was not soon forgotten that these were the liberties for which a war had been fought.

Knowledge of the Charter was not confined to England. The liberties, with slight changes, had been confirmed to Ireland. John's messenger in Rome at the time of the Lateran Council had made known "certain iniquitous laws and liberties," and had laid before the pope, "certain chapters of the aforesaid charter, reduced to writing." Prince Louis probably confirmed the Charter. He knew of the promised confirmation at the time of the Treaty of Lambeth, 1217. In 1223, when accused of violating this treaty, Louis reproached Henry III with not having kept the liberties which had been sworn to by all at the time of his withdrawal.

Publicity for the Charters must have been secured incidentally whenever the enforcement or interpretation of some particular provision was raised. Special orders to the sheriffs such as that of 1234 relating to article 35,[1] appeals in the courts, interpretation before the king's council—all such incidents must have served to emphasize the connection between any coveted privilege or procedure, and the great document which insured it. In addition to this incidental publicity, official treatment of the Charters did much to make known the documents and their contents, and to enhance their importance in popular estimation.

Treatment of Magna Carta differed from that of earlier char-

[1] Cap. 35 of the 1225 version, concerned with the session of local courts, included in the charter for the first time in 1217.

ters. A copy of the Charter of Henry I had been sent to each shire where it was to be kept in the most important cathedral church or abbey. The same procedure was probably used in regard to Stephen's charter of 1136, although there is less evidence that this was done; the provisions of Stephen's charter did not become well known. No orders appear in the records for proclaiming or reading these charters. In 1215 copies of Magna Carta were sent to the counties to be kept in cathedral churches or abbeys; but these copies were accompanied by letters patent to the sheriffs instituting an "inquiry into evil customs," and commanding enforcement of the Charter, "which we command be publicly read throughout your whole balliwick." This was the first order for a public reading.

The same procedure was followed in respect to the revisions of 1216, 1217, and 1225. In 1237, only the "little charter," confirming the Charters, was ordered read in country court. The Charter was read at the time of pronouncing the formal sentence of excommunication against violators of the Charters in 1253. This sentence was to be made public throughout the land. After Innocent's confirmation of the sentence reached England, the clergy were instructed to proclaim it, together with the papal confirmation. The sentence was repeated in 1255. This year, if not in 1253, orders were sent to all the sheriffs commanding them to observe the Great Charter, and to have the same read in full county court. The confirmation of 1265 prescribes "publication" of the Charters twice a year. The confirmations of 1297 and 1300 were accompanied by explicit directions for reading the Charters.

Professor Poole finds it difficult to believe "that so long and technical a document as Magna Carta could have been actually read aloud in Latin in the county courts."[2] He suggests that, in 1215, the procedure in the counties probably consisted simply of the oath-taking to the twenty-five barons, and the appointing of inquisitors. "No such conclusion, however, can be drawn from the mode in which Henry III ordered his first confirmation of the charter . . . to be proclaimed; for the writ which he issued to the sheriffs . . . contained only a command to cause the charter to be

[2] R. L. Poole, "The publication of Great Charters by the English Kings," *English Historical Review*, vol. 28, 1913, pp. 444–53.

read in the county court and the liberties contained therein to be firmly observed." Professor Poole suggests, then, some such procedure as that adopted for the Provisions of Oxford. Orders were given for the reading, not of the document itself, but simply of a short proclamation supporting the elective council and its work. Inasmuch as this proclamation was to be read in the common tongue, Professor Poole thinks that the reading actually took place in this instance. Yet it seems an unwarranted assumption that in the case of a brief document, the specific instructions of the government were carried out by the sheriffs, while in the case of the longer Charter of Liberties and of the Forest, equally specific instructions were disregarded.

The question arises, of course, what practical effect would be secured by reading the Charters in Latin to the average company of suitors at county court. Not until 1300 do the records state that the Great Charter was read *in English*. This reading of 1300, as described by the chronicler, took place in the great hall of Westminster before the archbishop and his clergy: the Great Charter, long desired, with all its articles, he ordered read before all who had come, "first in Latin, then in native tongue." The sentence of excommunication and papal confirmation of 1253 was to be read in both French and English; the Provisions of Oxford, in English. The same may have been done in the case of the Great Charter before 1300, but this can only be conjectured. Reading in Latin, would have meant something to any clergy present, and must have been impressive, if not instructive, to the lay element.

In regard to publication of the Charters, Professor McIlwain argues that publication in the county courts was an important part of the authentication of statutes.[3] "Only gradually did the theory arise that the whole of England was constructively in Parliament; that they were all assumed to be there consenting to what Parliament did." Again he says, "It is probable that some doubt existed in this period as to the reality of the assent 'of all parties' unless a statute had been actually proclaimed throughout the realm." Whatever part the theory of "assent" played in new legislation, it was evidently subordinate to that of securing *ob-*

---

[3] C. H. McIlwain, "Magna Carta and Common Law," *Magna Carta Commemoration Essays*, London 1917, pp. 122–179.

servance in the case of the Charters. Neither the provisions for publishing Magna Carta, nor similar orders in respect to private charters, mention securing recognition or assent. The command is always "you shall have proclaimed (or published or read) and kept." It was advantageous to have a law or privilege well known; then violations could not be excused on the plea of ignorance, or claims based on fictitious grants. This purpose is expressed in connection with lesser enactments and private charters. It is stated in some of the orders for publication of the Great Charter. The confirmation of 1265 provides for publication twice a year, "so that no one may pretend ignorance in future." The same idea is expressed in the order for enforcement of 1297 and 1300. With this object of publication in mind, it seems all the more probable that some reading of the Charters actually took place.

Not until 1265 was publication in the county courts prescribed as a regular proceeding. The proclamation of peace sent to the sheriffs in that year provides for publication at least twice a year, in the first meeting of the county court after Easter and after Michaelmas. Unfortunately there is little evidence of how well such an order was carried out in succeeding years, when there was no recent confirmation involved. The novel attempt at publicity for the Charter made by Archbishop Peckham in 1279, may indicate that the order of 1265 was not carried out year after year. In the Canons of Reading, the archbishop not only provides for excommunication of violators of the Charter, but orders that copies of the document, "well and clearly written," be posted in some prominent place in all cathedral and collegiate churches, the copies to be renewed from time to time. The plan must have been carried out in some churches, for Edward's order countermanding the canons provides, "Let Magna Carta be taken from the Church doors." Provision for reading the Charters in the churches was made in the *Confirmation* of 1297: "And we will that the same charters shall be sent under our seal to cathedral churches throughout our realm, and there remain, and shall be read before the people twice in a year." It was probably in accord with this order that Archbishop Winchelsea caused the Charter to be published throughout his province. The document had already been read at the October meeting of the council at Westminster in which the *Confirmation* was issued, and again at London. At this time, too, the sheriffs of London received orders to publish the Charter throughout the city. Walter of Heminburgh states that in 1299, when the barons were incensed at Edward's delay in carrying out any disafforestments, the king's counsellors, fearing an uprising, had copies of the Charters read publicly in St. Paul's cemetery before a large crowd of people. The most elaborate provision for publicity was made in the *Articles on the Charters:* "And that the Charters be delivered to every Sheriff of England under the King's seal, to be read four times in the year before the people in the full county court: that is to wit the next county court day after the feast of Saint Michael, and the next county court day after Christmas, and at the next county court day after Easter, and at the next county court day after the Feast of Saint John."

The whole policy of publication must have done much to bring the Charters to popular attention, and to acquaint the more intelligent elements in the community with their contents.

METHODS OF ENFORCEMENT

With the omission of article 61,[4] and the abandonment of any such means of control as the committee of twenty-five barons, the revised Great Charter contained no provision for its enforcement, or for the punishment of violators. From 1216 on, however, the Charters received the protection of the church through the great excommunication; and of the state through the ordinary courts, or some special group temporarily constituted "preservers of the liberties."

1. *Protection of the church, excommunication of violators.*— The practice of excommunicating violators of the Charters, or of pronouncing in advance a general sentence of excommunication to be incurred *ipso facto* by all who should infringe them thereafter, seems to have remained the only permanent general measure of dealing with charter-breakers throughout the thirteenth century. At first thought, the practice of excommunicating violators of a royal charter so largely secular in its application seems peculiar. The practice may be explained by the events of 1216–17, partly by the interest of the church in the Great Char-

4 Omitted in the 1216 and all subsequent versions.

ter. Ecclesiastical and papal support of the young Henry III had taken the form of excommunicating his opponents. These included persons who did not accept the compromise offered in the form of the revised Charters of 1216 and 1217. In 1225 there were no groups in open revolt against the king. There were some malcontents, some turbulent spirits among the barons, royal officials who were not observing the Charters, suspicion that the king himself, on coming of age, might not abide by his promises. Hence the custom established under ecclesiastical direction in 1216–17 was continued. This time, the sentence, pronounced by Stephen Langton, was directed primarily against possible future violators of the Charters. It was repeated in connection with the confirmations of 1237, 1253, 1255, 1276, 1297, and 1300, and at other times during the century.

Magna Carta, as the clergy interpreted it, really meant more to the English Church than any special papal or royal charter in their possession, for it guaranteed the sum total of all these, and other prescriptive and interpretative rights as well. It must be remembered, too, that the pope continued to look upon England as a fief of the Holy See. In the reign of Henry III, especially, papal direction in temporal affairs, persisted. Furthermore, it was not uncommon for the clergy to excommunicate "disturbers of the king's peace." The clergy were guardians of the temporal, as well as the spiritual, welfare of the kingdom. It was customary for them from time to time to pronounce general formal sentences of excommunication in which were included a number of prescribed offenses. These were largely offenses against the canons and the liberties of the church, but some secular items were often included. Such general sentences became somewhat stereotyped in form. Particular emphasis was put upon excommunication for any offense, when such a sentence had been sanctioned by the pope, or had been pronounced by some famous prelate, or upon some important occasion. Such was the sentence pronounced by Stephen Langton at the Oxford convocation of 1222 against all who should violate the liberties of the church. Such was the sentence against violators of the canons of the legate Cardinal Otto-boni, 1268. Such was the sentence against violators of the liberties of the church, and the liberties of Magna Carta and the Forest Charter, pronounced by Archbishop Boniface in 1253; sanctioned by Pope Innocent IV in 1254, and by Alexander IV in 1256.

From this time on, if not before, violation of the Charters was included as one of the offenses to be emphasized by the clergy in pronouncing their general sentences of excommunication.

The government, of course, recognized these sentences, either by the presence of king and counsellors at the ceremony, or in some more formal way. In connection with the sentence of 1253, a warning was issued against any attempt to introduce changes into it for "the lord king, and the aforesaid magnates, and the whole community of the people protested publicly" in the presence of the archbishop and bishops, "that they had in no wise consented or would consent to any such, but flatly contradicted them." The pronouncing of such sentences was formally prescribed in the *Confirmation* of 1297: "and that all archbishops and bishops shall pronounce the sentence of great excommunication against all those that by deed, aid, or counsel do contrary to the foresaid charters, or that in any point break or undo them. And that the said curses be twice a year denounced and published by the prelates aforesaid."

The effectiveness of this weapon as a preventative or penalty may be questioned. It was a failure as far as the king was concerned. In 1237 Henry III admitted that he himself had incurred the sentence of excommunication. In 1244 the barons complained that he had paid "no regard to the oath he had taken," nor shown "any fear of the sentence pronounced by the holy man Edmund." From time to time, Henry was supported by papal bulls, forbidding the clergy to excommunicate him, or his officials, directly. The Dunstaple Annals describe a case of excommunicating individual offenders for a specific offense: Roger, the prior of Christ Church, Canterbury, and those "by whose counsel the king despoiled him of the custody of the land of Ralph, son of Bernard, which belongs to his fief." But the chief offenders were exempted —"excepting the King and Queen, and Earl Richard and Stephen Segrave." The grievances of the clergy complain that the government releases excommunicated persons. When excommunication was used for secular offenses, and often against those that the government was glad to connive at, the weakness of the system is apparent. No doubt, some of the very persons released, "in contempt of the keys of the Church," were among the charter-breakers.

The clergy, however, continued to take the excommunication

of violators very seriously. In an age when the church still had a strong hold on men's lives and imaginations, the ceremony of excommunication must have been peculiarly impressive, and thus acted as a deterrent on some would-be violators. It is interesting to note that Archbishop Winchelsea recognized the value of the ceremonial side of the proceedings. In his letter to his clergy on the sentence of 1297, he orders them to use all ceremony and solemnity as this has more influence on the laity than the effect of the sentence.

The ceremony of 1253 is described as follows:

"This third day of May in the great royal hall at Westminster, in the presence and with the consent of our sovereign Henry, the illustrious king of England, and of their highnesses . . . we B[oniface], by the divine mercy, archbishop of Canterbury and primate of all England, Fulk, bishop of London . . . , clad in our pontifical robes, and with candles lighted, have solemnly pronounced sentence of excommunication, in the following terms, against all violators of the liberties of the Church, and of the liberties or free customs of the kingdom of England, especially those which are contained in the charter of the liberties of the kingdom of England, and in the charter of the forests. . . . 'By authority of the Omnipotent God, and of the Son, and of the Holy Ghost, and of the glorious mother of God, the ever-virgin Mary, of the blessed apostles Peter and Paul, and all the apostles; and of the blessed archbishop and martyr Thomas, and of all martyrs, of Saint Edward, king of England, and of all confessors and virgins, and of all the saints of God, we excommunicate, anathematize, and banish from the threshold of the holy mother Church, all those who shall by any arts or contrivances rashly violate, diminish, or change, privily or publicly, by word, deed, or counsel, the liberties of the Church, or the ancient and approved customs of the kingdom, and especially the liberties and free customs which are contained in the charters of the common liberties of England and of the forests, which charters have been granted by our lord the king of England to the archbishops, bishops and other prelates of England, the earls, barons, knights, and freeholders, by rashly contravening them, or any of them, in any article soever. Also, against those who shall promulgate, or, if promulgated, shall observe any statutes, or shall introduce, or, if introduced, shall observe any customs contrary to those liberties or their statutes; and against all writers of such statutes, as also the counsellors and executors of them, and who presume to judge according to them. And let all and singular the abovementioned persons, who shall knowingly commit any one of the aforesaid offences, rest assured that they will incur this sentence by so doing; and those who shall through ignorance so offend, and shall not, on being warned thereof, reform, and give full satisfaction for their offences within a fortnight from the time of admonition, at the discretion of ordinary judges, shall, from that time, be included in this sentence. In this same sentence, also, we include all those who shall presume to disturb the peace of the king and kingdom. In lasting memory whereof we have affixed our seals to these presents.' Then was brought before the assembly the charter of his father John in which he, the said king Henry, had, of his own free-will granted the aforesaid liberties, and was read to them."[5]

Whether or not the pious inclinations of the king were such that he was really impressed by the ceremony at this time, he had a faculty for lending himself well to a dramatic situation:

"The king, as he listened to the above sentence, held his hand to his breast, and preserved a calm, cheerful, and joyful look, and when at the end of it they threw down the candles, which on being extinguished sent forth a stench, and each and all exclaimed, 'Thus perish and stink in hell all who incur this sentence,' the bells at the same time ringing, he thus spoke, 'So help me God, all these terms will I faithfully observe, as I am a man, a Christian, a knight, and a crowned and annointed king.' At the commencement of pronouncing this sentence, it should be remarked, lighted candles were given to all present, and when one was handed to the king, he took it but would not retain it, and handed it to one of the prelates, saying, 'It is not proper for me to hold such a candle, for I am not a priest; the heart gives surer proof;' and for the rest of the time he held his open hand to his breast, until the sentence was ended."

5 The account is derived from the St. Albans chronicler Matthew Paris who repeatedly confused the various versions of the charter. The charter read out in 1253 was in fact the version of 1225.

This sentence the bishop of Lincoln had repeated in each parochial church in his diocese. The next year, the sentence, together with the papal confirmation of it, was sent to the clergy throughout England for proclamation, "clearly and lucidly in both English and French." With the text of the proclamation were sent copies of the Charters from which other copies were to be made (and the original returned).

This whole procedure of the great excommunication, then, familiarized the clergy with the text of the documents; it published abroad the names of the Charters in the impressive sentence which "aweth the heart, and whosoever heareth it, both his ears shall tingle." Some of the awe thus inspired must have been transferred from the sentence to the great document which occasioned it.

2. *Protection by the state.*—No formal pronouncement on the nature of secular punishment for violation of the Charters seems to have been made before 1265. In most cases, special methods of punishment were hardly necessary, for violations of those provisions of the Charter, classed as common law, would be dealt with in the appropriate feudal or royal court. This fact is evident from cases cited above in which appeals to the Charter were upheld in the courts. It is recognized in the *Confirmation of the Charters,* 1297: "and that our justices, sheriffs, mayors, and other officials which under us have to administer the law of our land, shall allow the said charters in pleas before them and in judgments in all their points; that is to wit, the Great Charter as the common law and the Charter of the Forest according to the Assize of the Forest, for the relief of our people." The same principle is expressed in the *Articles on the Charters,* 1300, but with the reservation that some parts of the Charters were not common law, and hence could not be upheld satisfactorily by the regular courts; and that adequate punishment for violators had not been provided heretofore: "Forasmuch as the Articles of the Great Charter of Liberties, and of the Charter of the Forest, . . . have not been heretofore observed or kept, because there was no punishment executed upon them which offended against the points of the Charters before mentioned; . . . And for these two Charters to be firmly observed in every point and article, where before no remedy was at the Common Law, . . ." The difficulty in securing proper observance of the Charters led to two practices during the

thirteenth century: first the custom of dealing with violators in the king's court; second, the creation, from time to time, of special committees to act as "preservers of the liberties."

The first practice, of course, was right in line with the whole development of the century in increasing royal jurisdiction. Threats of punishment of violators by the king's court are made in orders to the sheriffs, 1234, commanding observance of the liberties. In connection with the sentence of excommunication pronounced in 1253, it is made clear that in addition to incurring this sentence, offenders are to be proceeded against in the king's court. A formal declaration to this effect appears in the confirmation of 1265. Enforcement and punishment, either by the king, or by his officials, is provided by article 5 of the Statute of Marlborough, 1267: "The Great Charter shall be observed in all his articles, as well in such as pertain to the King, as to other; and that shall be inquired afore the Justices in Eyre in their circuits, and afore the Sheriffs in their Counties when need shall be; and Writs shall be freely granted against them that do offend, before the King, or the Justices of the Bench, or before the justices in Eyre when they come into those parts. Likewise the Charter of the Forest shall be observed in all his Articles, and the Offenders when they be convict, shall be punished by our sovereign Lord the King." The confirmation of the Charters in 1301, provided that the kind of violation which consisted of making new enactments contrary to the Charters, was to be dealt with "by the common counsel of our whole realm." A most novel procedure is that suggested by the author of the *Mirror of Justices:*[6] since every free man possesses a "free tenement" in the liberties of the Charter, he ought to be able to recover any of them which he has been denied, by a process of *novel disseisin!*

The second practice—creation of special groups to enforce the liberties and punish violators—was more or less a part of the whole constitutional struggle of the thirteenth century, the experiments in devising machinery of government to control the king. The twenty-five barons of article 61 were really "preservers of the liberties," although primarily against violations by the

6 *Mirror of Justices*, an inaccurate legal textbook written c. 1290, the source of many legal apocrypha, frequently used by Coke and other seventeenth-century lawyers as a statement of Anglo-Saxon law.

king. This committee, however, was not a judicial body; its weapons were confined to remonstrance and civil war. The plan of 1244 for a group of special counsellors to control the king, specified that these men were to be "preservers of the liberties": they were to be empowered to "hear the complaints of each and all, and, as soon as they can to afford relief to those who are suffering injury." One aim of the baronial government set up by the Provisions of Oxford of 1258 was to secure observance of the Charters.

The most complete scheme, and most interesting because it was devised expressly for securing observance of the Charters, was that prescribed in the *Articles on the Charters*, 1300: "And for these two Charters to be firmly observed in every point and article where before no remedy was at the Common Law, there shall be chosen in every shire court, by the commonalty of the same shire, three substantial men, knights or other lawful, wise, and well-disposed persons, which shall be Justices sworn and assigned by the King's letters patent under the Great Seal, to hear and determine without any other writ, but only their Commission, such plaints as shall be made upon any point contained in the foresaid Charters, in the shires where they be assigned, as well within franchises as without, and as well for the King's officers out of their places as of others; and to hear the plaints from day to day without any delay, and to determine them, without allowing the delays which be allowed by the Common Law. And the same knights shall have power to punish all such as shall be attainted of any trespass done contrary to any point of the foresaid Charters, where no remedy was before by the Common Law, as before is said, by imprisonment, or by ransom, or by amercement, according to the trespass."

None of these schemes was permanent; other experiments followed in the next reign. But publicity was given the Charters by these attempts. The very failure to secure adequate means of enforcement of the liberties necessitated the constant appeals to the documents, the repeated confirmations, which did much to perpetuate the Great Charter and its companion Forest Charter.

JUDGMENT OF PEERS: THE LAW OF THE LAND

12a FROM   *Magna Carta, 1215,*
                  cap. 39

12. Cap. 39, more than any other section of the charter, illustrates how recurrent interpretation ensured not so much the survival, but the regeneration of Magna Carta. The chapter is given under (a) below as it appears in the 1215 Charter. However, most references to it in the later middle ages or in the seventeenth century were to the version of 1225 confirmed in 25 Edward I. In this version the chapter is slightly amended and is associated with cap. 40; the two together are usually counted cap. 29. This version is given in (b). (c) is an early example of an appeal to cap. 39/29 by a knight. (d) is from Sir Edward Coke's Second Institute, *the text of which was impounded along with the rest of his papers by Charles I on Coke's death in 1634; it was published by order of the Long Parliament in 1641.*

---

39. No free man shall be taken or imprisoned or disseised or outlawed or exiled or in any way ruined, nor will we go or send against him, except by the lawful judgement of his peers or by the law of the land.

SOURCE. (a) See appendix.

12b FROM   *Magna Carta, 1225,*
cap. 29

No free man shall be taken or imprisoned, or disseised of any freehold of his or of his liberties or free customs, or outlawed or exiled or in any way ruined, nor will we go or send against him, except by lawful judgment of his peers or by the law of the land. To no one will we sell, to no one will we deny or delay, right or justice.

12c FROM   *The Year Books, 1302-3*

A certain Hugh, accused of rape, challenges the membership of a jury. [He has already been denied benefit of clergy and, since the charge is brought by the Crown, the advice of counsel.]

JUSTICE. Hence the court considers that you should answer as a layman and that you should agree to these honest men of the twelve because we know that they will not lie on our behalf.

HUGH. My lord, it is they who accuse me and therefore I will not agree to them. Moreover, my lord, I am a knight and should not be judged except by my peers.

JUSTICE. Since you are a knight we wish you to be judged by your peers.

And the knights were named and Hugh was asked if he wished to make any objection to them

HUGH. My lord, I do not agree to them. You may make any enquiry you wish *ex officio,* but I will not agree to them.

JUSTICE. Sir Hugh, if you will agree to them they may, with God's help, strive on your behalf. If you wish to reject the com-

SOURCE. (b) J. C. Holt, *Magna Carta,* Cambridge University Press, 1965, p. 355.

SOURCE. (c) *Year Books 30–31 Edward I,* ed. A. J. Horwood, Rolls Series London, 1863, pp. 529–32.

mon law you will bear the penalty imposed by it, namely "one day you shall eat and another day you shall drink; and on the day on which you drink you shall not eat and vice versa; and you shall eat unsalted barley-bread and drink water" *and he indicated fully to him that it was better to agree to them than die thus.*

HUGH. I will agree to my peers, but not to those twelve who have accused me, wherefore listen to my objections against them.

[The objections were heard secretly in gaol and accepted. The jury was reconstituted without the objectionable members.]

JUSTICE. We accuse Sir Hugh of the rape of a certain woman. He has denied the charge and, on being asked how he wishes to acquit himself has placed himself on the good testimony of the neighbourhood. Hence he has placed himself on you for good or ill. Whence we enjoin you on your oath to say whether Hugh raped the aforesaid woman or not.

THE TWELVE. We state that she was seized by force by Sir Hugh's men.

JUSTICE. Was Hugh a party to this or not?

THE TWELVE. No.

JUSTICE. Did they have carnal knowledge of her?

THE TWELVE. Yes.

JUSTICE. With or without her consent?

THE TWELVE. With her consent.

JUSTICE. Sir Hugh, they have acquitted you and therefore we acquit you.

12d FROM *Coke on Magna Carta cap. 39/29*

"No free man." This extends to villeins, saving against their lord, for they are free against all men, saving against their lord. . .

Concerning "liberties." This word, liberties, hath three significations:

SOURCE. (d) E. Coke, *The Second Part of the Institutes of the Laws of England,* third edition, London 1669, pp. 45–57.

1. First as it hath been said, it signifieth the Laws of the Realm, in which respect this Charter is called the Charter of Liberties.

2. It signifieth the freedoms, that the subjects of England have; for example, the Company of Merchant Tailors of England, having power by their Charter to make Ordinances, made an Ordinance that every brother of the same Society should put the one half of his cloths to be dressed by some clothmaker free of the same Company, upon pain to forfeit 10s. etc.; and it was adjudged that this Ordinance was against Law, because it was against the Liberty of the subject, for every subject hath freedom to put his cloths to be dressed by whom he will, and so on in similar situations. And so it is, if such or the like grant had been made by his [the King's] Letters Patent.

3. Liberties signifieth the franchises and privileges which the subjects have by gift of the King, as the goods and chattels of felons, outlaws and the like, or which the subject claim by prescription, a wreck, waif, stray and the like.

So likewise, and for the same reason, if a grant be made to any man, to have the sole making of cards, or the sole dealing with any other trade, that grant is against the liberty and freedom of the subject that before did, or lawfully might have used, that trade, and consequently against this Great Charter.

Generally all monopolies are against this Great Charter, because they are against the liberty and freedom of the subject, and against the Law of the Land.

"The law of the land." For the true sense and exposition of these words see the statute of 37 Edward III cap. 8 where the words "by the law of the land" are rendered "without due process of law". . . that is by indictment or presentment of good and lawful men. . . or by writ original of the Common Law. . . This chapter is but declaratory of the old law of England.

As the goldfiner will not out of dust, threads, or shreds of gold, let pass the least crumb in respect of the excellency of the metal; so ought not the learned reader to let pass any syllable of this law, in respect of the excellency of the matter.

13   FROM   *F. M. Powicke*
   By Judgment of Peers or the Law of the Land, 1917

Professor Sir Maurice Powicke, Regius Professor of Modern History in the University of Oxford 1928–1947, here investigates the contemporary meaning of cap. 39. His essay, which is reproduced in full, was written for the 700th anniversary of the charter; in large measure its conclusions still stand.

In his recent treatise upon the origin of the English constitution Prof. G. B. Adams has pushed to its logical conclusion what may be called the baronial tendency in current interpretations of the thirty-ninth clause of the Great Charter. The barons, he suggests, were thinking almost entirely, if not entirely, of themselves. They were demanding that they should not be imprisoned, disseised, or outlawed except after a trial in the King's Court "by the judgment of their peers and by the whole body of law and custom which such judgments are intended to interpret and apply."[1] By the King's Court the barons meant the magnates of the realm, not the judges alone; by the law of the land they meant no particular form of procedure, certainly not the processes of indictment and presentment As I understand this view, the barons desired to place themselves beyond the scope of the judicial system elaborated in the reign of Henry II and Richard I. They were thinking of such trials as those of William of Saint-Calais and St. Thomas of Canterbury.

This view is clear and intelligible. It is a good starting-point. Without traversing the whole field of speculation fully described in Mr. McKechnie's commentary,[2] I wish to put over against Pro-

[1] G. B. Adams, *The Origin of the English Constitution*, New Haven, 1920, p. 266.

[2] W. S. McKechnie, *Magna Carta*, Glasgow, 1905: 2nd edition, 1914.

SOURCE. *Magna Carta Commemoration Essays*, ed. H. E. Malden, London, The Royal Historical Society, 1917, pp. 96–121. Reproduced by permission of the Council of the Royal Historical Society.

fessor Adams' view the old fourteenth-century interpretation of the clause and see what can be said for it. There appears to be no doubt that, in the minds of politicians of Edward III's reign, the clause comprehended all freemen, and the law of the land covered all the due processes of law, even indictment and the appeal; whether there was a judgment of peers or not depended on the circumstances. We can all agree that the barons were thinking mainly of their own safety and were *not* thinking directly of trial by jury, but if we accept the Edwardian view, we cannot hold that the Charter is simply the programme of a pack of feudal reactionaries. According to Professor Adams the barons were seeking to undermine—so far as it concerned them—the whole fabric of the new judicial system, "including the jury, the itinerant justice court, and the permanent central Court of Common Pleas." According to the fourteenth-century politicians, the barons frankly recognized the value of the judicial system, new and old, and in this clause were maintaining the rights of the subject against an arbitrary prerogative.

The inquiry involves two separate but related questions. In the first place, assuming that the clause was intended to apply to the barons alone, was it only concerned with a trial by peers in the King's Court? In the next place, ought we to limit the phrase "free man" to the baron? If the barons were not thinking of the ordinary freeman, they may none the less have been thinking of more than one judicial method. If they did include the ordinary freeman in their demand, they would naturally allow a variety of procedure.

I

In cap. 39 the barons and their followers were included among the "free men." Indeed, John's letters of 10 May, 1215, show that the baronial desire for protection was perhaps the original motive of the clause. These letters, addressed a month before the date of the Charter, read as follows:

"Know that I have conceded to our barons who are against us that we shall take neither them nor their men nor disseize them nor go against them by force or arms except by the law of our realm or by the judgment of their peers in our court, until matters have been considered by four whom we shall choose from our side, and by four whom they shall choose from theirs, and by the lord Pope who shall be over and above them."

It does not appear, however, that the King is promising a trial by peers in his court as a remedy in all cases. Even though by the barons' men only their more important followers were intended, John is not likely to have given an undertaking that all charges against them would be brought before the supreme authority. Nor do the words "by the law of the realm or by judgment of peers," taken in their natural sense, suggest that the law of the realm and a judgment of peers are indissolubly connected or, in this case, identical. Such a serious conclusion must be based upon a much stronger argument than the probable meaning of "uel" (or). The word "uel" (or) is used about sixty times in Magna Carta, but never, so far as I can see, in an explanatory or a cumulative sense. However vague or weak its disjunctive quality may be, it cannot suddenly be construed as "et etiam" (and also) or "id est" (that is). As the author of the "Dialogus de Scaccario" points out, even "et" (and) was frequently used at that time in a disjunctive sense. Unless the meaning of the terms themselves suggests a much closer connection between the ideas of the "law of the realm" and the "judgment of peers," the use of "or" can only suggest that they are not rigid alternatives. One would expect the King to mean that, without stating exactly the scope of the law of the realm, he would observe it: it might include a judgment of peers or it might not; if the circumstances were peculiar—owing, for example, to the importance of the offender or the difficulty of the case—the judgment would not be arbitrary. The defendants' peers could be or would be called upon to see that justice was done.

The practice of the time and the general meaning of the words used strengthen the probability of this interpretation.

In many cases a judgment of peers in the King's Court was doubtless the normal method of procedure. A great baron's default of service, for example, might result in disseisin by such a judgment. But a judgment of peers was not the only legal way. During the sharp quarrel in 1205 between King John and William the Marshal, the Marshal offered to defend his fidelity against the most valiant man in the kingdom. "By God's teeth," swore the King, "that is nothing. I want the judgment of my barons." The Marshal was ready to stand this test also, but the barons shrank from giving judgment; and when John of Bassingbourn, one of the King's bachelors, ventured to speak, the Count of Aumâle silenced him. "It is not for you or me to judge a knight of the Marshal's quality. There is no man here bold enough to put his default to the proof of the sword." The duel is distinguished in this scene from the "judgment of peers"; the barons regard the duel as the more appropriate test, while the King prefers the "judgment."

Did the "law of the realm" mean the old form of procedure, such as the feudal trial by combat? Procedure was certainly part of the law of the realm; and some scholars have wished to limit the meaning of the phrases "law of the realm," "law of the land," to this form of trial, excluding any wider sense, e.g. process, and the methods of appeal and indictment which might precede the actual proof. I can see no reason for any such limitation in the thirty-ninth clause of the Great Charter. The "law of the land," which is substituted for John's "law of the realm," was certainly used of the ancient forms of proof, but in Norman and in Anglo-Norman law, it was more frequently used in the sense of the "general body of law operating through familiar processes." The word "land" was used sometimes to denote a holding as in the phrase "lands of the Normans," but also to denote a district subject to public law, whether the local "patria" or the "kingdom" as a whole. Its substitution for "kingdom" in the clause under discussion shows that "law of the land" was here intended to apply to the customs of England, and probably to cover also any varieties of local customs, such as those recognized by the justices in Kent and Herefordshire. And it may be noticed that the phrase "law of the land" was commonly used of actions and procedure generally; for example, of the possessory assizes, a writ of right, and the proceedings in outlawry.

The phrase "judgment of peers," on the other hand, had a more limited and precise meaning. It implied a particular kind of court, a court of doomsmen. The judgment must be delivered on behalf of a company of men who were of the same race or nationality or status as that of the accused or party. It involved the equitable principle which underlay the recognition and the accusing jury; indeed, the processes of inquiry and judgment met in the jury of arbitrators, of which we have an example in John's letters of May, 1215; but the judgment of peers was not the same as, and did not include, the recognition and the presentment. The Jews in England claimed the judgment of their peers, but they objected to a mixed jury of recognitors. A solemn trial in the King's Court in the presence of the magnates of the realm, the ordinary session of the shire court, perhaps also the trial of possessory actions before justices enforced by local knights involved a judgment by peers. The proceedings before the justices on eyre did not, I think, involve this kind of judgment. But the "law of the land" would be enforced in all alike.

A contemporary change in Norman procedure illustrates very clearly the distinction between the "law of the land" and the "judgment of peers." After the conquest of Normandy, King Philip Augustus took the trial of ducal pleas in the bailliwicks out of the hands of justices and gave it to local men. The custumal says: "assizes are to be held by barons and lawful men. Peer should be judged by peer."[3] The procedure of the court and the law enforced by the court were not affected by the change; the "law of the land" was observed both before and after; but henceforward a trial according to law would in Normandy involve a "judgment of peers." In England this was not necessarily the case.

The phrase "law of the land," then, though not excluding a judgment of peers, suggests so many varieties of law and procedure that a demand for a judgment of peers in every possible case could hardly be expressed in words so mild and general as "by judgment of peers or by the law of the land." I have pointed out that even a great baron accused of default did not regard the judgment of his peers as the most natural or obvious way of meeting the charge. Moreover, other clauses of the Charter indicate that the barons used more explicit language when they wished to emphasize a demand for a "judgment of peers." Disputes about land on the Welsh border were to be settled "by

---

[3] Peer has the general sense here of men of the same status, not the limited meaning of peer of the realm.

judgment of peers according to law," in accordance with the law of England, Wales, or the March, as the case might be.[4] The conclusion is forced upon my mind at least that the thirty-ninth clause was intended to lay stress not so much on any particular form of trial as on the necessity for protection against the arbitrary acts of imprisonment, disseisin, and outlawry in which King John had indulged.

If we turn to some leading cases of the next twenty years—a period during which the Great Charter was solemnly renewed, fresh in men's minds, and acknowledged as authoritative—this view is confirmed. There is the same insistence upon protection, the same concern for the observance of law, and also the same hesitation or indifference about the actual constitution of the court. The King acknowledges that he has disregarded the forms of law, it may be in his own court or it may be in a shire court. Redress is given by the magnates of the realm, if the case is of great importance, or by a judge in the royal following. Maitland was fond of reminding us that the distinctions between the royal courts were but vaguely defined in the thirteenth century; and with similar indefiniteness we find cases decided now by the assembled magnates, and now by a single justice.

One such case concerned a great Yorkshire house. The desirable manor of Cottingham, which had been much improved first by William, then by Nicholas de Stuteville, was claimed by Nicholas's co-heiresses on their father's death in 1233; but it had been for some weeks in the possession of his nephew Eustace, a man of some importance in the affairs of the shire. This was clearly a case for an assize of *mort d'ancestor,* and for a writ of right. For some reason the King intervened, dispossessed Eustace, installed the heiresses and their husbands, and finally ("by the counsel of the magnates of his court") took the manor into his own hands. Eustace had offered large sums for a judgment, and in 1234, at Wallingford, on the octave of Trinity (25 June), his claim was heard by William Ralegh. The King was present, and admitted that he had acted on his own initiative in disseising Eustace, without due process of law—"without summons and without judgment." Eustace was ready again with his offer of £1000. The fine was accepted, and judgment was given that he should be rein-

4 Magna Carta, caps. 52, 55, 56.

stated pending a settlement by assize of mort d'ancestor and writ of right, "according to the law of the land."

Eustace de Stuteville seems to have come to an arrangement with Hugh Wake, one of his rivals, and was clearly doubtful of his claim. But the King had disseised him without a judgment, and the decision at Wallingford points to the legal process by assize and writ, to a possessory and proprietary action, as the means of "summons and judgment." A thousand pounds was a large sum. Yet a royal admission of error in the royal court was perhaps worth the money. The case appears on a roll of "pleas which followed the King before W. de Ralegh." Eustace was apparently restored, not by "judgment of peers," but by one of the King's judges. The other claimants were disseised by an administrative act of their peers; but in Eustace's history there is no mention of such a judgment. Stress is laid, not on it, but on summons, judgment, assize of mort d'ancestor, writ of right, the law of the land.

A more famous trial of the same year illustrates the proceedings "by law of the land" in the case of outlawry. The decrees of outlawry declared by King Henry against the great Hubert de Burgh and also against Gilbert Basset and other companions of Richard, Earl Marshal, were annulled by a judgment of their peers, declared by the mouth of the same William Ralegh who decided the Cottingham case. The King, says the record, desired to show justice, and on 23 May, 1234, called together all the magnates then present in his court at Gloucester, including Edmund, Archbishop of Canterbury, bishops, earls, and others. This judgment ended the political crisis during which the Earl Marshal, before his violent death in Ireland, and Gilbert Basset had made the claim to be tried by their peers, and had been met by Peter des Roches with the well-known retort "There are no peers in England." One would expect, therefore, a deliverance by the court at Gloucester on the question as to whether a baron could be outlawed without a judgment of his peers. But the judgment contains nothing of the kind. It reverses the decree of outlawry in Gilbert Basset's case, (1) because the act which provoked the King (the rescue, namely, of Hubert de Burgh from sanctuary at Devizes) was done "in the course of war" and was not, therefore, an ordinary criminal offence; (2) because the proceedings of outlawry in the shire court of Wiltshire were irregular; and only in

the third place (3) because Gilbert and his friends had been prepared to stand their trial in the King's Court. The decree against
Hubert de Burgh was annulled on the ground that escape from
prison was not in itself punishable by outlawry. In both cases,
stress is laid on the proceedings in the shire court, that is to say,
on the "law of the land." The magnates clearly imply that these
barons, distinguished though they were, could have been lawfully
outlawed if they had fled "from a reasonable accusation, or from
a charge by the Lord King, acting on an accusation by the locality." Bracton, as Maitland points out, probably had this judgment in mind when he stated that outlawry at the King's suit or
command is a nullity unless an inquest has been taken by the
justices and the fugitive has been found guilty. Elsewhere Maitland describes the judgment in Hubert's case as an "important
step in constitutional history," since it made indictment or appeal
a necessary preliminary to outlawry. But was not the court simply
enforcing the principle laid down in the Great Charter? Was it
not interpreting the principle to mean that the "law of the land"
in a case of outlawry was the process in the shire court, involving
either the indictment or the appeal?

II

I have suggested that the barons did not claim a judgment of
peers as an essential and universal remedy even for themselves.
Their words do not imply this claim, and actual practice did not
enforce it. The "law of the land" might be trial by combat, as in
the Marshal's case in 1205, or proceedings in a possessory action,
as in Eustace de Stuteville's case, or indictment or appeal, as in
the case of Gilbert Basset and Hubert de Burgh; it did not involve a "judgment of peers." That was either an alternative or a
last resort, a solution of a judicial or political deadlock. But it is
not clear that the barons were thinking only of themselves.
Indeed, the conviction that this clause asserts a claim to the judgment of peers in all cases has, I think, been father to the thought
that the words "free man" do not include the ordinary freeman.
Students of the Charter have felt that a claim to the judgment of
his peers by the ordinary freeman was either unnecessary or
absurd. They have urged also that the barons had no special

interest in the judicial rights of the ordinary freeman, and in the manner of King Charles I liked to speak of themselves as freemen. The substitution of the words "free man" in the thirty-ninth clause for the "barons and their men" of King John's letters had no special significance.

First, let us look at the use of the words in the Charter. The freeman appears six times. In the fifteenth clause he is protected against unlawful and unreasonable aids levied by his lord; in the twenty-first against amercements which might shatter his social position; in the thirtieth against forced contributions of horses and waggons for carrying purposes; in the thirty-fourth against the loss of his court by a writ "praecipe"; in the thirty-ninth against arbitrary imprisonment, etc.; and in the twenty-seventh clause regulations are laid down for the distribution of his chattels if he should die intestate. If we set aside the thirty-fourth and thirty-ninth clauses for the moment, the Charter clearly safeguards the ordinary freeman; limits are set to the power of his lord; local officials are to respect his freedom; judges are to permit his neighbours to amerce him fairly; his relatives are not to suffer when he commits that last sin of intestacy. In two of these clauses the ordinary freeman is explicitly distinguished from the baron; in the twenty-seventh and thirtieth he is primarily intended. Is it credible that in the thirty-fourth and thirty-ninth clauses the same phrase, "free man" can exclude him?

Recent exponents of the Charter have not, I think, allowed sufficient weight to the fact that the document was not a baronial manifesto, but a carefully drafted statement of a settlement in which churchmen, citizens, and statesmen who had large experience of public affairs took part. Archbishop Langton and several of the barons on each side were not likely to overlook the growing significance of the freeman in English society, or the danger which the community of the realm would run if his economic and legal position were not protected. By the close of the twelfth century the freeholder was an important element in every feudal state of civilized Europe. In most countries it is probable that he did little more than represent a general economic tendency towards fixed services and money rents; and that affranchisement was a privilege of more or less sentimental value, not affecting the actual position of a serf. In England the freeman, however slightly his economic status might differ from that of the villein, was becoming essential to the state, as the state was more and more defined in laws and institutions. Within the economy of the manor, the freeman, or, to speak more accurately, the free tenant, strengthened the wealth and dignity of the lord. On the one hand, enfranchised villeins were founding families. On the other hand, as the "Domesday Book" of St. Paul's records, old tenements were frequently resettled, or new tenements divided, among free tenants paying fixed rents. It was to the common interest that these men should not be broken; and the thirty-ninth clause of the Charter, in protecting them and their tenements against illegal interference from the King and his officials, in my opinion simply applied the general principle expressed in other clauses.

We have seen that, in the case of outlawry, the "law of the land" required a charge either by indictment or appeal in the shire court. There is some evidence for the view that the thirty-ninth clause met in addition the desire of the freeman for protection against administrative proceedings at the King's command, and especially against imprisonment without the prospect of a trial in the local court. The contest between the principles of order and liberty had already begun. The natural instrument of order was the prison. During a political crisis or an epidemic of criminal unrest it was convenient to issue commands for a summary inquiry and for the imprisonment of suspected persons "during his Majesty's pleasure." The well-known royal edict of 1195, preserved in the chronicle of Roger of Howden, was in fact a command of this sort—a Crimes Act, disregarding the usual procedure. During King Richard's absence in the Holy Land the country had been much disturbed; and Hubert Walter, the new justiciar, was determined to restore order. The great inquiry of 1194 did not meet the situation: the justices had probably been too busy to get through the ordinary police business; indeed Roger of Howden tells us that a very important inquiry into the administration of sheriffs and local officials was postponed. Hence in 1195 knights were appointed to deal with crime. A sworn obligation was imposed upon all males of fifteen years and upwards. The inhabitants of each district swore that they would keep the King's peace, join in the hue and cry, deliver all who were guilty or suspected of robbery and theft to the knights appointed. The knights passed on the malefactors to the sheriff, who was "not to release them save at the command of the King or justiciar." The

duty prescribed to the King's subjects was very similar to that
which they performed in the hundred court, but the procedure
was different. The presentments were received by special commissioners, and the imprisonment of those presented followed as a
matter of course: "many men were seized and imprisoned in the
King's gaols," says Roger of Howden, "on the sworn testimony
of trustworthy men of the neighborhood." No mention is made
of judgment in the shire court before the justices. The trustworthy men were not the jury of presentment: and the accused
had no opportunity of alleging their general good character and
of submitting to the proof. It is probable that the ordinary
methods of attaching and trying criminals had broken down; they
broke down periodically during the Middle Ages; but they were
quite definite and must have been well understood. Suspected
persons were arrested by the sheriff and his bailiffs, sometimes by
the tithing man or in the hue and cry. They might be locked up
in the King's gaol or entrusted to the custody of the tithing; or
they might be handed over to their relatives or pledges who
would be made responsible for their appearance. They were
presented, whether in captivity or not, at the sheriff's tourn, and
again at the shire court before the justices on eyre. If they were of
bad repute and had been arrested in the act, they might be
punished according to the discretion of the court without further
inquiry, that is to say, without going to the ordeal or other proof;
yet even in such a case the Assize of Clarendon (1166) admitted
the right of the accused to find a surety—"if he cannot find a
surety let him have no law." Other suspected persons, those, for
example, of decent repute who had been found in possession of
stolen goods, went to the ordeal and, after the abolition of the
ordeal, were given the opportunity of placing themselves "on the
neighbourhood," of standing by the verdict of a jury. In all this
process imprisonment was merely an incidental affair; it was not
yet a common form of punishment after conviction, and only
gradually became so general as a form of detention as to neces-
sitate commissions of gaol delivery.

The distinction between the normal procedure and the drastic
action taken by Hubert Walter in 1195 was to be of the greatest
importance in future history. Was it realized at the time?

At first sight the answer seems to be decidedly in the negative.
It is not likely that any opposition was made to the particular

edict of 1195; the royal duty of good government included the
maintenance of the public peace. These malefactors were persons
of ill fame and were arrested after sworn inquiry among their
neighbours. Whether they were tried or not in the future would
be a matter of general indifference and could be left to the royal
discretion. Moreover, the King was the source of justice; "the man
committed to gaol 'on the order of the Lord King' would," in the
twelfth and thirteenth centuries, "have found none to liberate
him." By Bracton's time a sheriff who released on surety a man
who had been arrested by the King's command or on the command of the justiciar would have defied the law of England; and,
although this rule, it is true, applied to prisoners awaiting trial,
there was nothing to compel the King to bring them to trial.

It must be admitted that administrative action such as Hubert
Walter's was regarded as within the lawful scope of authority;
also that persons imprisoned by the King's command could, before the law of *habeas corpus* had been painfully hammered out,
be tried at the King's pleasure. The royal edict of 1195 is the first
of a long series of formal acts, enforcing what may be termed the
"administrative law" of the prerogative—a prerogative which still
exists in King and Parliament. Yet I believe that, even at the
close of the twelfth century, the desire to emphasize the extraordinary nature of this reserved power was both felt and expressed.
This desire is expressed, I think, in the thirty-ninth clause of the
Great Charter. The Charter did not succeed in abolishing the
prerogative right of imprisonment—it was more successful in
stretching the protection of the law over the free tenement—but
it did assert the principle that the freeman must normally be
accused and punished in a special manner, however awkward or
inefficient that manner might be.

From the days of Henry II, the two methods of keeping the
King's peace—the one "by the law of the land," the other by administrative action—may be traced in mediaeval England.

1. It is clear that Henry II anticipated the action of Hubert
Walter, probably with much less formality. The proof is to be
found in the action of Queen Eleanor after Henry's death in 1189.
She sent commissioners through England to liberate prisoners.
The orders given to these commissioners carefully distinguished
various kinds of persons who were in gaol. Offenders against the

forest law were to be set free and pardoned. Persons imprisoned "by common law" were to find pledge for their appearance in case an appeal should be brought against them; if they could find no pledge, they were to be sworn to appear. Various other classes who had been subject to legal process were also enumerated; they were in most cases to be released under conditions. But one group was, like the offenders against forest law, to be freed unconditionally:—

"All those who were seized and held by will of the King or his Justice and are not detained by common law of shire or hundred or by appeal, are to be free."

Clearly, in 1189 the King's prisons contained persons who had been imprisoned by decree, not in accordance with the procedure defined in the Assizes of Clarendon (1166) and Northampton (1176). Unimportant people who should have been presented at the hundred court had not escaped Henry's attention. However salutary this direct intervention may have been, it was felt to be anomalous; in order to show that a new reign had begun the Queen Mother declared an act of grace.

2. Two years later restrictions were imposed by the barons on the justiciar's power of administrative disseisin. The critics of William Longchamp admitted the right of the King to disseise a vassal of his property without a rigid observance of the new procedure; but as a rule the lawful customs and assizes of the kingdom must be observed:

"It has also been conceded that bishops, abbots, earls, barons, knights and free tenants are not to be deprived of their lands or chattels at the will of the Justices or other ministers of the Lord King, but are to be dealt with by judgment of the court of the Lord King according to the lawful customs and assizes of the realm or by mandate of the Lord King."

Two points are noticeable in this passage. The free tenant, who is distinguished from the baron and knight, was explicitly included; and protection was particularly desired from the royal officials. The demand was extended in Magna Carta 1215, to protection against the King, and was defined still more clearly in Magna Carta 1217, in a passage which recalls the wording of this treaty:—

"No free man . . . shall be disseised of any freehold of his or of his liberties or free customs, . . . except by lawful judgment of his peers or by the law of the land."

3. Disseisin was more easily dealt with than imprisonment. We have seen that, between 1189 and 1215, Hubert Walter systematized the practice of imprisonment "on the mandate of the King," and forbade release "except by the King or his chief Justiciar." In John's reign, this practice, recognized as anomalous in 1189, became a nuisance. John was for one thing not concerned to take the opinion of his victims' neighbours into consideration: he was after booty, not justice. He spared neither small nor great; and he was compelled to surrender this prerogative in 1215. As Mr. McKechnie has reminded us, later opponents of the jurisdiction of the King's council interpreted the thirty-ninth clause of the Charter in this way. They insisted upon the necessity of indictment or presentment by good and lawful people of the neighbourhood in which the crime was committed. Coke borrowed the same construction from Edward III's statutes when he translated "by law of the land" by the words "due process of law." The phrase, indeed, is a very fair equivalent to Queen Eleanor's "by common law of shire and hundred or by appeal." On this view the clause comprehended the criminal procedure of the twelfth century. It said in effect: "Unless the case is so anomalous or the accused so important that a trial in the King's Court by the magnates of the realm is desirable, he must be dealt with in the usual way, by presentment or indictment, in hundred or shire courts with recourse to the customary proofs."

4. Neither baron nor freeman got matters all his own way. In the thirteenth century we have "state-prisoners" who did not find much help in Magna Carta. In 1241 the sheriffs were instructed by Henry III to keep suspected persons "in our prison until you receive further instructions from us." In 1264 Simon de Montfort went further than Hubert Walter had gone in 1195. In the King's name he placed every shire under a single "keeper of the peace," who was instructed to use the whole strength of the shire for the arrest of criminals and disturbers of the peace; the arrested persons were to be kept in custody "until we order otherwise." But Simon's action was taken under very abnormal conditions. On the whole, the principles laid down in the Charter were observed

with remarkable continuity. I have already pointed out how Henry III was obliged in 1234 to reverse an unlawful disseisin and the unlawful outlawry of certain barons. The freeman was also protected. The royal officials, for example, had reason to be very prudent and circumspect in their dealing with suspected persons: a rash imprisonment might involve them in heavy damages. The periodic revival of disorder, in fact, was encouraged by the conditions which made officials and communities alike unwilling to prosecute their duties—a false step was so expensive. The Government tried to deal with disorder by reforms in the police organization, but did not—except on rare occasions, as in 1241 and 1264—interfere with procedure. The police reforms were no more an infringement of the Charter than was the growth in the practice of imprisonment pending trial, or the rule that a man so imprisoned by the King's command could not be replevied. Yet these reforms have probably been confused with the occasional edicts interfering with the "law of the land," although in reality they maintained continuity in procedure. The thirteenth century conservators of the peace, whether they were serjeants elected by the shire, or knights appointed by the King, or important barons invested with special powers, were concerned mainly with the "view of arms" and the process of arrest. Just as the headboroughs and constables kept the peace in township and manor, so the conservators assisted the execution of the common law in hundred and shire. The elaborate writ of 1242, which assigned knights in each shire, refers explicitly to the subsequent trial of suspected persons "by law of the land," thus correcting the action taken in the previous year:—

"The sheriffs shall take into safe custody, without difficulty or delay, all suspects by whomsoever they have been arrested, until they are released by law of the land."

One of the objects of the Statute of Winchester, which codified previous legislation in 1285, was the more conscientious and exhaustive presentment of malefactors by the local juries. The conservators were gradually given judicial functions and developed into the justices of the peace; but they still administered the common law—the "law of the land." Hence, when Stubbs traced a connection between Hubert Walter's "appointed knights," Earl Simon's "keeper of the peace," and the justice of the peace, he

was, I venture to think, suggesting a misleading confusion between the exceptional and the normal in the history of criminal
law. So far as their police duties were concerned, the connection
between these officials is clear, but it is easy to forget that, whereas
the justice of the peace had behind him the Assizes of Arms (1181)
and Clarendon, the officials appointed in 1195 and 1264 had not.
The peculiarity of the measures taken in 1195 and 1264 lay, not in
the method of arrest, but in the imprisonment during the King's
pleasure. The commissions issued to the justices of the peace,
on the contrary, from the period when they combined the
functions of conservators and justices until the year 1590, directed
the enforcement of the Statute of Winchester, that is to say, of
the final definition of the system laid down in the Assizes of Arms,
Clarendon and Northampton. The justices were so circumscribed
by the "law of the land" that in the fifteenth and sixteenth centuries they could not order an arrest until the accused had been
indicted in "open sessions of the peace." In Edward III's reign
the practice was more elastic, but well within the limits of the
traditional system. According to the commission of 1357 the justices were to arrest after inquiry "by sworn testimony of honest
and lawful men," and to determine the cases "according to the
law and custom of our realm of England." The statute of 1360
ordered them to pursue, arrest, and punish evildoers "according
to the law and customs of the realm."

The "law of the land" constantly broke down in the time of
justices of the peace as it had constantly broken down in hundred
and shire. The difficulties are described clearly in the Statute of
Winchester, and in the petitions to the judges on eyre, to council,
to the chancellor, and to Parliament. The folk of the district
would not present, officials grew slack and corrupt. The justices
in their turn were too often either overworked or open to unjust
influences. In the twelfth and thirteenth centuries, the King's
ministers or council tried to remedy matters by decrees for laying
criminals by the heels; in the fourteenth the council began to
hear and determine petitions on its own account—began, in
short, to lay the foundation of that judicial control which was
later to develop into the Courts of Star Chamber and Requests.
It was under these new circumstances that Parliament, appealing
to the Great Charter, raised its voice on behalf of the "law of the
land," the system of indictment and presentment. The party of

law, not for the last time in our history, was not the party of order, even though it was the party of progress.

In the fourteenth century the important phrase was "law of the land"; in the seventeenth the party of law and progress fastened on the phrase "judgment of peers." In this paper I have tried to show that, however badly the contemporaries of Pym and Selden may have blundered, there is a good deal to be said for their fourteenth-century predecessors. In 1215 neither baron nor freeman was concerned primarily with a judgment of peers so much as with justice. The "judgment of peers" ran through a good part of English procedure, but was not universal. From the baronial standpoint it was especially important as a last resort, in cases where justice had not been done, and the law was uncertain. The barons had no intention of excluding from the "law of the land" any part of the new judicial system, neither the Court of Common Pleas, nor the justices in eyre, nor the presentment of the grand jury. They were demanding, as they demanded at Merton in 1236, that the practices of English law should not be changed. In the same spirit they desired that sheriffs and other local officials should be men acquainted with the "law of the realm."[5] And on the whole they got their way. The peculiarity of English history is not that the common law is supreme, but that it is so practised as to seem supreme, and that other expressions of the sovereign power—whether the equitable jurisdiction of the King's Council in the fourteenth century or a Defence of the Realm Act in the twentieth—are universally admitted to be temporary and abnormal. If King John had not grossly abused his power as the source of justice, it is quite possible that this tradition would never have been formed. The policy of efficiency practised by men like Hubert Walter, Thomas Cromwell, and Francis Bacon might well have gathered momentum and swept aside the prejudices in favour of the Common Law.

[5] Magna Carta, cap. 45.

14   FROM   *Faith Thompson*
                   Magna Carta, 1948

*Professor Thompson here examines the development of cap.
39/29 especially of the phrase "law of the land" in the fourteenth
century.*

"For mine own part, I shall be very glad to see that old, decrepit
Law *Magna Charta* which hath been kept so long, and lien bedrid, as it were, I shall be glad to see it walk abroad again with
new vigour and lustre, *attended and followed with the other six
statutes*; questionless it will be a great heartening to all the people." Thus Sir Benjamin Rudyerd spoke in the course of the
famous 1628 debates on "liberty of the subject." The so-called
six statutes were fourteenth-century interpretations of Magna
Carta chapter 29, ranging in point of time from 5 to 42 Edward
III. They were used by counsel for the five knights; formally
grouped with the Great Charter in one argument by the commons in conference with the lords, April 7, 1628; cited as the
six statutes in succeeding debates; and partly incorporated as
precedents in the Petition of Right.

Legal historians have shown that the writ of habeas corpus, as
a safeguard to liberty of the subject, did not derive from Magna
Carta or from any medieval device such as the writs *de odio et
atia*[1] and *de homine replegiando*,[2] but rather from various writs
of habeas corpus in use as procedural writs. Nevertheless, Holdsworth believes that it was the happy (if historically unjustified)
connection of the writ of habeas corpus with the Great Charter,
effected in the seventeenth century, which made possible its later
benevolent role:

[1] Writ *de odio et atia*: writ requiring a jury to determine whether an
appeal had been made maliciously "out of hate and spite."

[2] Writ *de homine replegiando*: writ for the release of a prisoner on
surety.

SOURCE. Faith Thompson, *Magna Carta, Its Role in the Making of the
English Constitution 1300–1629*, University of Minnesota Press (c) 1948. Reprinted by permission of University of Minnesota Press.

"Whether or not the famous clause of Magna Carta, which enacted that 'no free man shall be taken or imprisoned or disseised or exiled or in any way destroyed except by the lawful judgment of his peers or by the law of the land,' was intended to safeguard the principle that no man should be imprisoned without due process of law, it soon came to be interpreted as safeguarding it. Because it was interpreted in this way, it has exercised a vast influence both upon the manner in which the judges have developed the writs which could be used to safeguard this liberty, and upon the manner in which the Legislature has assisted that development. Without the inspiration of a general principle with all the prestige of Magna Carta behind it, this development could never have taken place; and equally without the translation of that general principle into practice, by the invention of specific writs to deal with cases of its infringement, it could never have taken practical shape.[3]

The writ of habeas corpus thus needed the support of the Great Charter. It may be suggested that the latter, to be effective for this purpose, needed the support of the *six statutes*. Had the Charter "walked abroad again" unattended by the "other six statutes," could it have been used as effectively as it was? "For these words 'by the law of the land,' " said Noy, "what 'law of the land' should be, I will not take upon me to expound, otherwise than I find them to be expounded by acts of parliament; and this is, that they are understood to be the process of the law, sometimes by writ, sometimes by attachment of the person." Similarly Littleton, "Out of this Statute I observe, that what in *Magna Charta,* and the Preamble of this Statute [25 Edward III, chapter 4] is termed by *the Law of the Land* is, in the Body of this Act, expounded to be *by Process made by writ Original at the Common Law,* which is a plain interpretation of the words *Law of the Land* in the Grand Charter."

The various interpretations of chapter 29 among which the *six statutes* are to be found, occur usually as commons petitions (or statutes based on such petitions) protesting the jurisdiction and procedure of the council, or the summary procedure of special commissions, and in Richard II's reign (1377–1399), of the

[3] W. S. Holdsworth, *History of the English Law*, London 1926, vol. 9, p. 104.

Court of the Constable and Marshal. A few individual petitions also take exception to the Exchequer as a non-common-law court. The petitioners are not concerned with the "judgment of peers" either in the technical sense or in the sense of trial by equals or trial by jury; in fact the phrase is usually omitted in the partial quoting (or misquoting) of chapter 29. It is rather the magically elastic "by the law of the land" which is invoked to secure trial in common-law courts, and by routine common-law procedures such as original writ or indictment.

Both parliament and the lawyers distrusted the jurisdiction of the council. It was "identified with the crown and the prerogative." It not only exercised a competence outside the common law but tended to encroach on the field of the latter. It was feared for its power and disliked for the very efficiency of its procedure. Furthermore, "the council took up criminal cases on 'information' or 'suggestion' by whomsoever it was offered. This was a mode of accusation that was creeping in as the earlier method of criminal appeal declined. It differed from the appeal in that it was unaccompanied by any challenge to battle; it might be offered either publicly or secretly, and without traditional safeguards. . . . the danger of the system lay in its being applied on the slightest suspicion and even falsely and maliciously." This practice was especially resented. As a result the jury of *presentment* was becoming valued as a jury of *indictment*—a safeguard against false accusation. It is in this period (the 1360's) that Miss Putnam finds the juries in quarter sessions, in addition to their presentments, certifying individual complaints or bills with the now familiar "This is a true bill."[4]

As to special commissions, parliament and the administration differed over personnel and powers. It was hard to strike a happy medium between the weakness and inefficiency of local keepers or justices of the peace preferred by the commons and the strong-arm methods of commissions staffed with administrative officials and "great men" favored by king and council. Every student of the parliament rolls is familiar with the alternation of complaints of lawlessness and miscarriage of justice with protests against the methods devised to deal with these very evils. The remedy was

---

4 *Proceedings before Justices of the Peace in the Fourteenth and Fifteenth Centuries*, ed. Bertha H. Putnam, The Ames Foundation, London, 1938.

worse than the disease. Miss Putnam has worked out in detail the ups and downs of this conflict throughout the fourteenth century. The mediocre talents and services of local men, justices of the peace, were preferred to commissions granted to "distinguished lawyers, or to magnates and lawyers." The use of specially strong commissions was naturally revived in times of special disturbances such as the peasants' revolt and Jack Cade's rebellion.

Attempts to restrict the holding of common pleas in the Exchequer had been made in 1284, 1300, and 1311. It was the second of these, the *Articles on the Charters,* chapter 4 (based on Magna Carta chapter 11, not 29), that was to be remembered and used in later years. Yet certain individual petitioners in the 1330's do direct the magic "law of the land" clause against the Exchequer. They protest the action of a chamberlain in impleading them in that court for trespass (as his privilege of place entitled him to do), thus "cunningly contriving to maliciously aggrieve them and to deprive them of the common law." The first group (a prior, a chaplain, two monks, and one other) while not ignoring the "fixed place" for common pleas, base their case mainly on the right of free men to the common law: it is contained in the Great Charter "that no free man shall be taken, imprisoned, disseised, etc. except by the judgment of his peers or by the law of the land," and they show the king "that they were free men and ought to be treated according to the common law of the land."

Other jurisdictions encroaching on the field of the common law may be noted briefly. A series of statutes, of which again the *Articles on the Charters* (chapter 3) was the most fundamental, defined and restricted the jurisdiction of the Steward and Marshal for the king's household "within the verge," especially as to common pleas, but I have found no protests against this court based directly on Magna Carta. More opposition was aroused by the Court of the Constable and Marshal. A military court nominally under the control of the constable and marshal was in existence at least as early as the reign of Edward I. By the reign of Richard II this court had "developed apace." As the duel of law declined, the treason duel of chivalry made its appearance. French influence, the pleasure of the king and of such nobles as delighted in the splendid rites at royal expense, and, later in the reign, the increasing extension of the prerogative were responsible. The restrictive statute of 13 Richard II best defines what the proper jurisdiction of the court was thought to be, yet as the same statute complains, the court has encroached and "daily doth incroach Contracts, Covenants, Trespasses, Debts, and Detinues, and many other Actions pleadable at the Common Law, in great Prejudice of the King and of his Courts, and to the great Grievance and Oppression of the People." But according to Vernon-Harcourt the business of the court increased: "it took cognisance of actions for debt 'on grounds of breach of faith,' and also continued to deal with appeals of treason and felony on practically the same simple and comprehensive pretext. . . . From and after (if not before) the reign of Richard the Second the proceedings seem to have been exclusively in accordance with the civil law. Trial was by witnesses, or failing sufficient evidence, by battle."

From the Westminster parliament of 1331 comes the first of the group later to be dubbed the *six statutes*:

"It is enacted, that no man from henceforth be attached by any Accusation, nor forjudged of life or limb, nor his lands, tenements, goods, nor chattels seised into the king's hands against the form of the Great Charter, and the law of the land."

It has no corresponding petition in the incomplete record of the parliament roll for this session. It may have been prompted by the arbitrary regime of Isabella and Mortimer. . . .

The second of the *six statutes* (25 Edward III, statute 5, chapter 4) emanated from the same parliament which enacted the famous Statute of Treasons, 1352. This act follows almost verbatim one of the commons petitions; it is a clear-cut protest against the practice of accusation by "suggestion" to king and council, and is the most explicit exposition thus far of the "law of the land":

"Whereas it is contained in the Great Charter of the Liberties of England, that none shall be imprisoned nor put out of his freehold, nor of his liberties or free customs, unless it be by the law of the land; it is accorded, assented and stablished, that from henceforth none shall be taken by petition or suggestion made to our lord the king, or to his council, *unless it be by indictment of good and lawful people of the same neighbourhood where such deeds be done, in due manner, or by process made by writ orig-*

inal at the common law; nor that none be out of his liberties nor of his freeholds, *unless he be duly brought in to answer, and forjudged of the same by the course of the law*; and if anything be done against the same, it shall be redressed and holden for none."

A similar enactment (1354), much briefer in compass, constitutes the third of the *six statutes*. In this instance Magna Carta is not cited, but the provision follows close upon a confirmation of the Charter (chapter 1). In these acts of 1352 and 1354 the "free man" of the Charter has become in one case simply "none," in the other "no man of whatever estate or condition he may be." The second uses the phrases "in due manner or by process made by writ." The third is the first instance I have found where *due process of law* occurs in connection with chapter 29. Three years later the Charter is being invoked to secure "due processes" for "divers men of Ireland, great and small":

"Whereas certain of our justices of Ireland have arrested, taken and imprisoned divers men of Ireland Great and Small, by Writs, Precepts, Bills, and otherwise, at their Will, and without Indictments, Presentments, or due Processes, and have detained them in dark Prisons and bound in fetters, until through Duresses, Imprisonments, and Pains inflicted, they paid Fines and Ransoms to the Justices and their private Counsellors and Brocagers according to their Pleasure, to their own personal Profit and not ours, against the form of the Great Charter and other our Statutes thereupon made, and against the Law and Custom of the said Land; . . . We will and stedfastly command, that men being our Subjects, without Indictments, of Presentments, or other due Processes, against the form of the Charter and statutes aforesaid and the Law and Custom abovementioned, by our Justices of Ireland for the time being, or their Lieutenants, or by their Precepts, or Commands, or by Bills, shall by no means be taken nor imprisoned. . . ."

"Against the form of the Great Charter and *other statutes thereupon made*"—here is evidence that the latter are beginning to serve as precedents. This phrase recurs in 1362 and 1363.

In their selection of a fourth interpretation of chapter 29, counsel for the five knights made a bad blunder. Their 36 Edward III, number 9, is a general confirmation of the Charters and has

nothing to do with arbitrary arrest, as Attorney General Heath
ably demonstrated. The common lawyers were on surer ground
in citing another petition of the same parliament. To be sure,
this did not appear on the statute roll, but, as Digby said, it is
"the answer to the petition which makes it an act of parliament."
Certainly it must have had an especial appeal in 1627 and 1628
for it protests arrest by special command. Their fifth statute,
1363 (again based almost verbatim on a commons petition), not
only complains of false suggestions to the king himself, contrary
to the process of the law of Magna Carta, but provides that
henceforth such accuser find sureties before the council, and "if
his suggestion be found evil," incur the same penalties the accused would have suffered.

It is interesting to find that the last of the *six statutes*, 42 Edward III, chapter 3, was cited in cases of the nineteenth and
twentieth century. "This is treated by the Supreme Court of New
Zealand as a statutory prohibition of commissions of inquiry as
to offenses committed; and is also relied on by the counsel for
the University of Oxford." Actually here the commons were not
complaining of commissions but of false accusers who made their
accusations rather for vengeance or their own profit than for
that of the king or his people, and that persons thus accused
were brought before the council by writ or other command of
the king under heavy penalty, apparently the writ of subpoena.
Following a summary statement of the grievance, the statute pro-
ceeds in the identical words of the last part of the petition:

"It is assented and accorded, for the good governance of the
commons, that no man be put to answer without presentment
before justices, or matter of record, or by due process and writ
original, according to the old law of the land: and if any thing
from henceforth be done to the contrary it shall be void in the
law, and holden for error."

Neither petition nor statute cites Magna Carta, but both follow
almost immediately after a confirmation of the Charters, and are
followed (chapter 4) by a regulation as to irresponsible and abu-
sive commissions of inquiry. In the parliament roll the king's
answer reads: "since this Article is an Article of the Great Charter the King wishes that it should be done as the petition asks."
What more did the seventeenth-century interpreters of "law of
the land" in Magna Carta need than this?

This, the last of the *six statutes,* is also the last in the series of petitions giving specific content to the "by the law of the land" of chapter 29 which find a place in the statute roll. There are, however, a few petitions of allied character in the reign of Richard II. These protest respectively "false suggestions," overpowerful commissions, expanding jurisdiction of the Court of the Constable and Marshal, and some form of extralegal procedure. In the Gloucester parliament of 1378 the commons complain of a particular kind of false suggestion: persons intimate that certain lands are in the king's hands and then buy patents to have the same, thus ousting people from their freeholds to their great damage and disinheritance, "without redress and contrary to the form of the Great Charter."

Yet it was this same parliament which attempted to cope with the more than usual disorders in the country, especially in Wales and the western shires, by confirming the statute of Northampton and providing for special commissions of "sufficient and valiant persons, lords or other," with power over offenders "to arrest them incontinent without tarrying for indictments or other process of the law," and to have them detained in gaol until the coming of the justices "without being delivered in the meantime by mainprise, bail, or in other manner." This law was repealed in the very next parliament. The commons had protested it as "very horrible and dangerous for the good and lawful people of the realm," likely to result in misinformations and false accusations against persons by their enemies, or through the ill will of the commissioners themselves, "the which ordinance is openly against the Great Charter, and divers statutes made in the time of the progenitors of our lord the king, that no free man can be taken nor imprisoned without due process of law." At the same time another petition protests that persons are being appealed by bill before the constable and marshal for treasons and felonies done *within* the realm, imprisoned against the law of the realm "and against the form of the Great Charter, which wills that no man be imprisoned nor in any manner distrained except by the lawful judgment of his peers and the law of the land."

Again at the end of the reign, one of the charges incident to Richard's deposition reveals the abuses to which the Court of the Constable and Marshal was being put. After a recital of chapter 29 it accuses the king of having willfully committed perjury in violating this, one of the statutes of his realm: by his own command persons have been maliciously prosecuted for scandalous words against the person of the king, seized and imprisoned, and led before this military court, where they were allowed to make no answer except not guilty, and must defend themselves with their bodies against adversaries young and strong, although the accused were old, weak, maimed, or infirm.

After 1379, throughout the remaining twenty years of Richard's reign, chapter 29 falls into comparative oblivion. There are two exceptions, both interesting for their free "gloss on the text." Oddly enough the first comes from the Lords Appellant, in accusing Nicholas Brembre, "false knight of London," of having traitorously encroached on royal power in taking some twenty-two prisoners from Newgate, and having all but one beheaded at the "foul oak" in Kent, without warrant or process of law. The charge begins with a free rendering of chapter 29 appropriate to the occasion:

"Item this that according to the Great Charter and other good laws and customs of the realm of England 'no man shall be taken, imprisoned or put to death without due process of law . . .' "

There are a few other petitions of parliaments of Richard II and of Henry IV, V, and VI, protesting some aspect of the jurisdiction of the council, its use of letters of privy seal and the prerogative writs and subpoenas, but they no longer cite chapter 29. The practice in question is merely said to encroach on the common law; no resulting enactment appears on the statute roll, and the answers recorded in the parliament roll are evasive or qualified with reservations.

One more voice is raised in 1415, the voice of the "good people of Sandwich," who plead for the common law against the jurisdiction of the constable of Dover Castle in a dispute arising in connection with the trade with Flemish merchants. Their quaint petition, extremest example of a free rendering of the Charter, shows how far, in this age no less than in later centuries, one could depart from the letter yet hold to the spirit of the old law:

"May it please your honourable lordships to consider the following matter and also the statute of the Great Charter, which provides that no man shall be judged except by the common law, and also as is ordained in other statutes of ancient date, that no one shall be molested or troubled without due process of law. . . ."

As was usually the way with medieval legislation, no one en-actment produced definitive results. There was the inevitable re-affirmation and amplification, the pleas for more effective enforcement. Holdsworth concludes that these statutes did have one important result: "They prevented the Council from dealing with questions of freehold which were properly determinable by the common law courts by the machinery of the real actions; and they prevented it from dealing with questions of treason or felony, a conviction for which involved the death penalty and escheat or forfeiture of freehold." On the other hand they did not effect any essential alteration in the procedure of the council. Nevertheless, chapter 29 had certainly been made to mean more things to more people, to connote the later "liberty of the sub-ject." The next steps were to come rather incidentally through the compilers and printers of the statutes.

15 FROM   *Helen M. Cam*
        Magna Carta—Event or Document?

*The following is part of a commemorative lecture delivered by
Dr. Cam, Zemurray Radcliffe Professor in the University of Har-
vard, 1948–1954, to the Selden Society in July 1965. It carries the
development of the myth into the seventeenth century.*

___

When and how did this myth of the venerable immemorial
inheritance come into being?

In the first place it should be noted that unlike earlier charters
granted to the community both John's and Henry's charters were
granted in perpetuity. "For us and our heirs in perpetuity" is the
wording of John's Charter, while Henry's in 1225 runs "We have
granted all the following liberties to all the free men of the
realm to have and to hold to them and their heirs from us and
our heirs in perpetuity." A royal grant which contained no reference to the king's heirs would not endure beyond the grantor's
life.

Even so, kings had been and were again to be absolved from
their oaths, and their subjects sought to make assurance doubly
sure by securing solemn confirmations, for which they were prepared to pay by money grants, as for instance in 1225, 1253 and
1297, and to strengthen which they secured the support of the
Church by solemn and periodical excommunication of those who
infringed the Charters. During the long reign of Henry III such
renewals grew more frequent as the political atmosphere grew
more heated. It is noteworthy that Stubbs' description of the
reigns of Henry and his son as "The Struggle for the Charters"
is accepted by Stubbs' harshest critics, Richardson and Sayles.
Thus the Charters were confirmed at Oxford in 1258, after Lewes
in 1264, after Evesham in 1265, at the end of the Barons' War
in 1266, and most solemnly in 1267, when the Statute of Marl-

SOURCE. Helen M. Cam, *Magna Carta—Event or Document?* Selden Society,
London, 1965, pp. 17–26. Taken from Selden Society Lecture and reprinted
with permission.

borough recorded "It has been provided by the great council of ourselves and our magnates that the liberties contained in our great charter shall be observed on our part and on the part of others of our realm in every particular." It was through these struggles and renewals that the Charter was coming to be regarded as more than a safeguard of private and particular rights; as a symbol of not so clearly defined liberties for all. For the proclamations and excommunications read in the shire-courts all over the country served as publicity and propaganda. In 1253 the Charter was to be read both in French and English; in 1265 twice a year. The Church, whose liberties were guaranteed in the first clause of the Charter, lent its support not only by excommunication; one archbishop ordered a copy of the Charter to be posted in every cathedral; another ordered that it should be read out first in Latin and then in the mother tongue.

The culmination of the struggle for the Charters came in the years 1297–1300. It would seem that Edward I's barons aimed at incorporating in the now sacrosanct document new clauses limiting the right of the Crown to levy taxation without consent. The *Confirmation of the Charters* which they extorted from Edward in 1297 made such a concession, but neither this document nor the later *Articles on the Charters* attained the sacredness of the Charter, and though it was most solemnly confirmed by Edward in 1300, he obtained from the Pope in 1305 absolution from his oath to observe the new concessions.

Edward I's barons had failed in their attempt to bring the Charter up to date, and it is from 1300 onwards that its inadequacy to cover the main political issues of the times is becoming evident. The demands of the baronial opposition are no longer focused on the Charters. The famous Ordinances of 1311, in which the barons renewed against Edward II the attacks they had made against his father, are concerned mainly with the powers of the baronage in council and parliament, and the references to the Charter are incidental. But they are significant. The Ordinances provide that obscure points in the Charter are to be interpreted by the Lords Ordainers; and they declare that all statutes are to be observed *unless they are contrary to the Charter*. In 1301 Edward I had granted that statutes contrary to the Charters should be null and void; and though this may have been nullified by the papal bull of 1305, and the Ordinances of

1311 were revoked in 1322, the conception of the Charter as fundamental law was gaining ground. A statute of 1368 declared that any statute contrary to Magna Carta should be *ipso facto* null and void. But this accords little with reality; there is no record of the repeal of any statute on such grounds. Magna Carta is coming to be the symbol of the whole body of law, common and statute law, revered as a whole, though constantly modified in practice by judgment and legislation. The numerous confirmations of Edward III's reign are not political events, but routine procedure: every parliament opens with the petition that "the Great Charter and the Charter of the Forest, and all other statutes made in the time of the king's progenitors and in his own time be kept and maintained in all points." And it is noteworthy that although there is no reference to the Charter in any known version of the Coronation oath, Edward II's lawyers asserted that to infringe Magna Carta would be contrary to the oath taken at his Coronation, and Richard II in his first parliament was reminded that he had been charged at his Coronation to keep and observe the said Charter in all its points.

But alongside the removal of the Charter from the centre of political controversy to a remote sanctity there was taking place a most important development in the interpretation of one of its more ambiguous clauses. Clause 29 had provided that—

"No freeman shall be taken or imprisoned or disseised of his freehold or liberties nor shall he be outlawed or exiled or in any other way destroyed, nor will we go against him or send against him save by the lawful judgment of his peers or by the law of the land."

In the early fourteenth century the citation of this clause in particular cases, and its interpretation by the terms of new statutes, both enlarged its scope and defined its meaning. The internecine conflicts of Edward II's reign were punctuated by political trials and judgments, reversed by the opposite parties when they in turn came to the top. Thus in 1322 the process against the Despencers was revoked "as not in accordance with cap. 29 of Magna Carta." In 1327 the judgment on Thomas of Lancaster five years before was asserted by his brother Henry in parliament to have been erroneous "because he had been adjudged to death in time of peace without arraignment or being put to answer by the lawful judgment of his peers, contrary to the great charter of liberties," and the judgment was annulled by the king and magnates and the whole community in parliament. And in the following year archbishop Meopham, reminding the young king that in his Coronation oath he had promised to observe the laws and customs of the kingdom, pointed out that it was contained in the Great Charter that the king would not send against nor go against any man save by process of law and the judgment of his peers, whereas he—or rather Mortimer acting in his name—was taking up arms against Henry of Lancaster.

In these instances clause 29 had been adduced on behalf of magnates, and it was in their interests that judgment of peers was claimed and allowed in 1330 and 1340. But its benefits were not by now limited to aristocrats, if they had ever been. As early as 1302 a royal justice had interpreted it to entitle a knight to have his case tried by a jury of knights.[1] A statute of 1330 declared that no man shall be attached or forjudged of life and limb against the form of the Great Charter and the law of the land, while a statute of 1354 extended its protection to the unfree as well as the free by providing that "no man of what estate or condition soever shall be put out of his land or tenement or taken or imprisoned or put to death without being brought to answer by due process of law."

It is this phrase "due process of law" that comes to replace the formula "by the law of the land," and is destined to become sacred to Englishmen and to their descendants overseas. The statute of 1354 is one of a series running from the fifth to the forty-sixth year of Edward III, all of them aimed against new practices which were held to be contrary to established law. Some refer, as in Thomas of Lancaster's case, to trial without being "put to answer"; others to arrest without indictment or due process by writ original; others again to arrest by special mandate without presentment. Their originators, undoubtedly the common lawyers who were members of parliament, were fighting against the extension of the jurisdiction of the Council, with its summary methods and prerogative writs. They did in fact succeed in limiting the judicial functions of the council to cases which did not involve the loss of life or limb or freehold. The "Six Statutes" of

[1] See item 12 (c) above.

Edward III in effect rewrote clause 29 so as to secure to all Englishmen the protection of common law procedures in such cases, leaving available to them in civil litigation the more elastic equitable procedures which economic developments called for.

If clause 29 was given new life in the parliament of the fourteenth century, the Charter itself seems, as we have seen, to be merging into the body of the common and statute law. It is not named in the charges brought against Edward II in their depositions; its confirmations, from being perfunctory, grew less and less frequent—thirteen under Richard II, six under Henry IV, two under Henry V, and then they cease. As Bémont says, "The Great Charter rested in the shade from Henry VI to the Stuarts," or in the more vigorous words of Sir Benjamin Rudydre "That good old decrepit law of Magna Carta hath been so long kept in and lain bedrid, as it were."

It has often been remarked that Shakespeare's *King John* makes no reference to Magna Carta, any more than the older play on which it is based. But this does not mean that the common and statute law was not prized under the Tudors. It was held in deep respect, and Coke—

"blessed God for Queen Elizabeth, whose continual charge to her justices was that for no commandment under the Great or Privy Seal should common right be disturbed or delayed; this [he said] agreeth with the 'to no one will we sell' etc—the ancient law of England declared by the Great Charter."

But he is writing retrospectively; the resurrection of Magna Carta to which his *Reports* and *Institutes* so greatly contributed, did not come till the seventeenth century. He was, as Mr. Hill says, the great myth maker.[2]

Why the English went historical and dug up the Charter is a fascinating problem. There certainly was a popular vogue for reading national history in the late fifteenth century, as is attested by the great number of manuscripts of the *Brut* Chronicle, and when the printing press appeared, popular chronicles were among the earliest publications. But more significant for the study of medieval history was the sixteenth century taste for anti-

2 J. E. C. Hill, *The Intellectual Origins of the English Revolution*, Oxford, 1965, pp. 225–265.

quarianism, signalised first by the appointment of Leland as King's Antiquary in 1533, and later by the foundation of the first Society of Antiquaries in 1572, which met weekly for the discussion of records till it was suppressed in 1604. The press was making generally available collections of statutes, including of course the Charter of 1225, translated into English; Parker was printing medieval chronicles, and the substance of Matthew Paris's, published in 1571, was popularised in English by Holinshed and Stow a few years later. By the end of Elizabeth's reign, alongside the solid contribution that scholars like Lambarde and Spelman were making to early English history, there was growing up a legend of the ancient liberties of England before the Norman Conquest which was to be the seventeenth century version of the laws of Edward the Confessor.

Raleigh, writing his *Prerogative of Parliaments* in the Tower under James I, spoke of "digging from the dust the long buried memory of the subjects' former contention with the king," and cast into dialogue form the rival views of Magna Carta as "fostered and showed to the world by rebellion" and as part of the statute law "to which all men are bound by choice and self-desire." The association between historical research and politics thus indicated was to reach its height towards the end of James I's reign, when the house of Sir John Cotton, that great collector of medieval manuscripts, in Palace Yard, became the meeting place of scholars like Selden and Coke with Eliot, Wentworth and Pym, for discussion of the matters about to be raised in the House of Commons. But well before then Magna Carta was emerging from the shade of which Bémont speaks.

The lawyers had never completely lost sight of the Charter, and it was above all Coke who was responsible for reintroducing it into politics. The Case of Impositions in 1610 was the first occasion in which it was cited in parliament in connection with the powers of the crown. It was contended that clause 30 of the Charter limited the king's power to add to the ancient customs, and Coke further maintained that the Charter forbade the taking of any money except by parliamentary grant. The courts did not admit either argument, nor will they bear historical scrutiny. As Mr. Hill says, Coke interpreted Magna Carta lovingly, but inaccurately, and the great oracle was echoed by other parliamentarian lawyers in the panegyrics I cited above. The Myth of

Magna Carta had come of full age; and by a perverse paradox, the historians had helped to create it. Up till now the lawyers had relied correctly on the Charter of 1225, but the memory of John's Charter had never died. It had been cited by Henry III's barons in 1255. Copies of the Charter of Runnymede had been preserved alongside Henry's Charter in medieval collections of statutes. But now in the seventeenth century study of Matthew Paris, who declared that the Charters of 1215 and 1225 were identical and had supported this untrue statement by concocting a mongrel version containing clauses from both Charters, had led excellent scholars such as Selden and Brady to accept Paris's version as coming from a contemporary, "who was also the king's chronologer." The all important clause 29 of 1225 was practically identical with clause 39 of John's Charter; but the famous clause about no taxation save by the common council of the realm, dropped in 1216, figured, in a shortened form, in Paris's mongrel Charter, and as we have seen, was relied on by Coke in 1610. It was cited again by Selden in the case of the Five Knights, committed to prison for refusing to pay the forced loan, and by Oliver St John, in Hampden's case, to prove the illegality of Ship money. The depth of Matthew Paris's sins as a historian have only been plumbed in the twentieth century. Professor Holt has shown conclusively that he had access to authentic versions of both John's and Henry's Charters, but chose to obscure the facts. He remains, alas, the most readable as well as the least reliable of medieval chroniclers. His interpretation of thirteenth century history was accepted by most nineteenth century historians, including the great Stubbs, and has done more than anything else to create the traditional picture of John. And his garbled version of the Charter held the field until Blackstone set the texts to rights in 1759.

From 1610 onwards the lawyers are constantly citing Magna Carta both in the courts and in parliament; for instance in connection with the powers of monopolists, with the jurisdiction of the Marshalsea and the Star Chamber, with the impeachment of Buckingham. Clause 29 was expounded at length by Ashley in his Reading in the Middle Temple in 1618.

Respect for Magna Carta was common ground for king and parliament. Charles himself accepted its authority. But the crux of the matter was how its clauses, above all clause 29, were to be interpreted. The Five Knights' case in 1627 brought the matter to a head—was commitment "on special mandate of the King" contrary to clause 29 of Magna Carta? The issue had been raised in the parliaments of Edward III, but not determined. As Attorney-General Heath said "There is not a word of commitment of the King or commandment of the Council in all the statutes and records." The Ordainers who in 1311 had claimed for themselves the right to interpret the Charter had anticipated the conflicts of the 1620s. In 1621 the Commons had introduced a bill "for renewing of Magna Carta"—specifically for securing the subject against wrongful imprisonment contrary to clause 29 of Magna Carta—but it failed to reach the Lords. Now in 1628 when the Five Knights' case had raised the two basic issues of non-parliamentary taxation and extra-judicial commitment, Coke introduced a bill "to explain Magna Carta and put it in execution." In the long drawn out debates in the Commons, and in the Conference between the two Houses as to the meaning of "the law of the land," in which Selden and Coke were the chief spokesmen for the Commons, and in the exchanges between king and parliament, six different ways of handling the question were put forward. Charles offered to confirm the Charter and the "Six Statutes," but refused to accept an act of parliament curtailing his prerogative. But he finally agreed to Coke's suggestion that the two Houses should join in a Petition of Right to the King, that should declare the law in definite terms. And to this petition, read three times in each House, Charles assented in an *ad hoc* formula. *Soit droit fait comme est désiré*—"Let right be done as is desired." It was not a statute, but a declaration of law binding on the judges. The first clause, asking that no man be compelled to make any gift, tax or loan not imposed by parliament cites the statute *concerning not conceding Tallage,* the accepted Latin version of the *Confirmation of the Charters* of 1297, which Coke had described as "but an explanation of this branch of Magna Carta." The second clause, asking that no man be imprisoned or detained without cause shown, quotes Magna Carta c.29, and also the statute of 1354 that had first used the phrase "due process of law"; and the clause against martial law cites both the Charter and the statute of 1352—the second of Edward III's "Six Statutes."

With the granting of the Petition of Right Magna Carta ceases to be a battlecry. Henceforth the struggle was to centre on the powers of parliament, rather than on the liberty of the subject, and if that comes in question, it is the Petition of Right that is cited. Its last appearance is in the preamble to the Act abolishing the court of Star Chamber. It is not mentioned in the 1689 Bill of Rights. It has become a legend and a symbol.

But if in England Magna Carta was becoming quiescent, across the Atlantic it was taking on a new lease of life. Just as Selden and Coke were expounding the significance of the Charter to their contemporaries in the *Epinomia* and the *Reports,* the first settlers in the North American colonies were setting forth. What has been called the great Puritan migration—the crossing of the Atlantic by 20,000 colonists—was taking place in the years between the Petition of Right and the meeting of the Long Parliament. Cromwell, by his own account, would have been one of them if the Grand Remonstrance had not been carried in 1641. And by removing to America, as Franklin was to say, British subjects did not lose their native rights. A generation earlier the first colonial charter had declared that the colonists "should have and enjoy all liberties as if abiding in England," and the emigrants of the 'thirties were not likely to undervalue what Coke had described as "the inheritance of every subject—the law and custom of England." Of that law and custom Magna Carta was the chief embodiment. Thus for the young Commonwealth of Massachusetts one of their first necessaries was "to frame some body of the grounds of law, in resemblance to Magna Carta." These "fundamentals of the Commonwealth," the *Body of Liberties,* accepted as law in 1641, provided that—

"no man's person shall be arested, restrayned, banished, nor any wayes punished . . . , no mans goods or estaite shall be taken away from him . . . unless by vertue of some express lawe of the country warranting the same"

an obvious echo of cap. 29. The Maryland Assembly in 1638 had passed a bill to recognise Magna Carta as part of the law of the province. The code of laws for Rhode Island in 1647 was prefaced by cap. 29 of Magna Carta. Quotations from or echoes of the Charter occur in the laws of S. Carolina, Virginia, Pennsylvania and New Jersey. And as in England, the notion that Magna Carta forbade taxation without consent crops up; in New York in 1680 taxation was resisted as illegal, being "contrary to Magna Carta and the Petition of Right."

And when after the Declaration of Independence the thirteen Colonies set to work to frame their own constitutions, each included a bill of rights to secure the liberties of the citizens of the new states; and every one of these contained in one form or another the essence of cap. 29 of the Charter, usually in the form of Edward III's interpretative statute "that no person should be deprived of life, liberty or property without due process of law," though the Virginian Bill of Rights reads "except by the law of the land or the judgment of his peers."

Thus inevitably when the fathers of the Constitution completed their work by framing the Bill of Rights in 1791, what Bryce called "the legitimate child of Magna Carta" was written into the fundamental law of the United States in the words of the Fifth Amendment—"Nor shall any person be deprived of life, liberty or property, without due process of law." Generally speaking, the Bill of Rights is particularly concerned with the invasions of personal liberty which the American Colonists had suffered from the English Government in the years before independence, but the phrase "due process of law" derives from a far older tradition. Again in 1868, when the supremacy of the Union had been vindicated, the Fourteenth Amendment provided that "no *state* shall deprive any person of life, liberty or property, without due process of law."

What the rule of law means for Englishmen, what due process of law means to Americans, is inseparably bound up with our traditional notions of Magna Carta. Whether all that has been read into the document is historically or legally sound, is not of the first importance; every historian knows that belief itself is a historical fact, and that legend and myth cannot be left out of account in tracing the sequence of cause and effect.

If I may return to my original query, is it an event or a document that we are celebrating? the answer must be, it is both. When we honour Magna Carta today we call to mind the circumstances in which it was first framed and the circumstances which kept the memory of Runnymede alive; we recall the age-long association of the document with resistance to undue authority, with the protection of individual liberty, and with the preservation of traditions of law and custom older than the document itself, and we recognise the decisive importance of the revivification of that association in the seventeenth century. In the light of seven and a half centuries of English history Magna Carta is no archaic curiosity. It stands for something alive, as precious to us today as ever it was to our ancestors. It is all very well to say that the sovereignty of Parliament is the key to our Constitution. No constitutional lawyer, be he Dicey or Jennings, can leave it at that. If, as Maitland said, Magna Carta embodies the rule of law, we can say—as Coke said, though not exactly as he meant it— "Magna Carta is such a fellow that he will have no sovereign."

PART THREE

Comparisons
Charters of Liberties in Medieval Europe

16 FROM *J. C. Holt*
Magna Carta, 1965

*The following passage is concerned with the continental par-
allels to Magna Carta. It points to some of the general causes
which produced "charters of liberties" in western Europe between the late-twelfth and early-fourteenth centuries.*

Twelfth-century England had no constitution. There was no
general system of government in which powers were balanced,
functions allotted and defined, rights protected, and principles
stated or acknowledged. Instead there were the materials from
which a constitution of some kind might ultimately and in-
directly be compounded. Government was evolving routine procedures, methods which it found convenient to use in most, but
not necessarily all, circumstances. It operated in a society in
which privilege seemed to be part of the natural order of things:
privilege attached to this or that particular status, or privilege
which individuals held as a result of royal favour, or privilege
which great corporate institutions held as necessary conditions of
their function. From these primitive elements to a settled constitution was a long, tortuous and often bloody journey in which
the grant of charters of liberties was but one, and that an early,

SOURCE. J. C. Holt, *Magna Carta*, Cambridge University Press, 1965, pp.
19–24. Reprinted by permission of Cambridge University Press.

step. It was nevertheless a hazardous step, one which required determination and organization on the part of those who demanded and received such grants, and one which was necessitated by the power and complexity of the administrative machine under the control of those who granted them. It was a step which required considerable sophistication on the part of both, for it involved a fusion of the government's routine on the one hand with the privileges of the subject on the other. On the one side, routine procedures which the government had hitherto developed as administrative and political convenience dictated were now being conferred as rights to which the subject was entitled. On the other side, the privileges which the subject had hitherto enjoyed because of status, grant or prescription were now being extended to cover administrative procedures which were often of recent origin, which were never the exclusive concern of one particular subject, which might not be the concern even of one particular grade within the feudal hierarchy, and which could only be held by the recipients in common, in some kind of corporate capacity. All this required a refined political theory, subtler and more searching than that provided by the simple concepts of feudal allegiance; and the need was all the greater since the recipients of these grants of liberties never brought themselves to think outside the terms of reference prescribed by the society in which they lived, in which monarchical government, more or less immediate, was the basic component of any polity. Hence, in seeking liberties they required their kings to promulgate acts of self-limitation in which they agreed to restrict their own freedom and initiative, apparently of their own free will. This not only led the seekers and grantors of liberties into vigorous and prolonged argument. It also meant that a grant of liberties was never so secure that it ceased to be a matter of debate and political friction. Liberties forgotten were liberties dead.

Magna Carta was intimately connected in this way with developing political theories of the twelfth century. It was also a direct product of war. It was occasioned directly by failure in war, by the loss of Normandy in 1204 and by the defeat of John's ambitious campaign in Flanders and France in 1214. If the Charter had any single predominant source, it is to be found in the manner in which the Angevin kings of England exploited their realm in an attempt to expand and defend the continental empire of which England became a part with the accession of Henry of Anjou in 1154. Indeed, war, the emergence of international systems of alliance, the development of war economies, of advanced methods of taxation and other forms of fiscal exploitation, were just as characteristic of the twelfth century as were the political ideas stemming from the cathedral schools, the newly emerging universities and the everyday practice of the courts. War was the compulsive urgency behind administrative experiment and in the hundred and fifty years before the Charter England had had a full measure of this compulsion. But England was no exception in twelfth- and thirteenth-century Europe, and Magna Carta was far from unique, either in content or in form. In 1183, as part of the Treaty of Constance, the Emperor Frederick Barbarossa ended an unavailing war in northern Italy by granting the towns of the Lombard League a series of liberties which gave them practical independence of imperial rule. In 1188 King Alphonso VIII of Leon, in the midst of a long feud with Castille, promulgated ordinances in the *cortes* of Leon which conferred important feudal privileges on his vassals. In 1220 the young Emperor Frederick II bought support for his bid to unite the Empire and the Sicilian kingdom by granting special privileges to the ecclesiastical princes of the Empire. In 1222 King Andrew II of Hungary ended a period of expensive adventures abroad by granting the Golden Bull to his vassals. Nine years later Frederick II's son, Henry VII, found it necessary to quieten opposition in Germany by expanding and adding to his father's concessions of 1220 and extending them to the secular princes of the Empire; his father, increasingly embroiled in the affairs of Lombardy and Italy, confirmed the grant within a year. In 1282-3 the War of the Sicilian Vespers compelled Charles of Anjou and Charles of Salerno, on the one hand, to issue reforming ordinances in a bid to recover Sicily and stave off rebellion in southern Italy, and on the other forced the invader of Sicily, Peter III of Aragon, to buy support for an expensive foreign policy by conceding the *Privilegio General* to his subjects. There was only one striking exception in thirteenth-century Europe to this regularly repeated association of war with the concession of liberties, and that was the Capetian monarchy of France. In this case continued success staved off the inevitable retribution for foreign adventure until the next century when the exhaustion of French resources in the Aragonese crusade and the campaigns in Flanders eventually showed that France was no exception. Philip IV's great reforming ordinance of 1303 was here but a preface to the various provincial charters which his successor, Louis X, was forced to concede in 1315.

This reiteration of the same story throughout western Europe carries obvious implications. There was nothing particularly striking or extraordinary in the fact that King John had to end a period of disastrous wars in 1215 with the grant of a charter of liberties to his subjects. Magna Carta reflected English conditions, just as the *Privilegio General* did those of Aragon or the Golden Bull those of Hungary, but it did not spring from any insular genius, nor was it more searching or more radical than its continental parallels. A dispassionate observer in the thirteenth century would have attached no greater significance to the Great Charter than to the Golden Bull or the *Privilegio General,* nor would he have predicted that the English grant would in the long run have the greater influence. In the early years of the fourteenth century, indeed, such an observer would probably have shown no great surprise that many rulers throughout western Europe had at some time found it necessary to make such grants. To him grants of liberties would have seemed to embody the natural reaction of feudal societies to monarchical importunity. If he were a royal servant of a cynical bent he might have reflected that they were one of the probable costs of administrative inventiveness and efficiency. And indeed this paradox epitomizes the long and tangled conflicts which produced these liberties, for those same actions whereby kings overhauled and improved the government of their realms were often regarded by their subjects as tyrannous invasions of ancient right and custom.

In England the Norman and Angevin kings followed three such broad lines of policy. First, they exploited many of the functions traditionally attached to feudal lordship as financial resources for their wars and as instruments of political discipline to compel support, and to stave off and defeat rebellion. Secondly, they vigorously developed new methods of administration which lay quite outside the relatively primitive systems of government which elementary feudal relationships subsumed. Finally, to execute their policies, they created an establishment of "king's men" who owed power and position to efficient service of the Crown. These were policies typical of the west European monarchies at this time, but in England they were particularly telling. England was wealthy enough to be worth exploiting, small enough to be exploited efficiently, and was controlled by kings whose powers were in part derived from conquest. Elsewhere in Europe such conditions existed only in Sicily, and the parallel between the two was emphasized for contemporaries by the fact that the conquerors of both came from Normandy; both realms played vital rôles in international politics, the one in northern, the other in southern Europe; both were the centres of empires and of imperial dreams and ambitions. Yet the kings of England had advantages even compared with their Norman counterparts in Sicily, for the circumstances of the Norman conquest ensured that their settlement of England bore the tenurial imprint of their English and Scandinavian predecessors. The resulting rarity of compact and distinct territorial baronies deprived the Anglo-Norman aristocracy of one of the most important conditions for the maintenance of honorial justice and administrative and political resistance to the pretensions of the Crown. Moreover, the scattering of the lands of the king through almost every shire in the land meant that royal influence was ever-present. Everywhere in western Europe the royal demesne and the exercise of royal justice marched hand in hand; the second was rarely exercised effectively far from the bases which the first provided. Hence the tenurial structure of Anglo-Norman England ensured the supremacy of the royal sheriff over the aristocratic bailiff; it facilitated the rapid penetration of civil jurisdiction by royal justices and royal procedures, so that within a century of the Conquest the baronial courts were already surrendering to the advantages of a centralized and efficient exercise of jurisdiction; and it enabled the Crown to enforce its demands for aid and service throughout the land. It also meant that rebellion in defence of aristocratic privilege and alleged or actual baronial prerogative was from the start deprived of that secure base which compact baronies provided; even at an early date English rebels aimed not at excluding the king's government but at controlling it. When, under Stephen, Geoffrey de Mandeville and his like sought hereditary shrievalties and justiciarships they were giving implicit recognition to this inherent strength in the position of the Crown; outside marcher territory the cause of aristocratic independence, pure and simple, was not even stillborn; it was inconceivable. Hence while the demand for liberties on the continent was aimed at municipal independence, as in Lombardy in 1183, or at aristocratic immunity, as in the German concessions of 1220 and 1231 or the French charters of 1315, in England it was aimed at the control and subjection of the administrative functions of the Crown. These came to be regarded, not as competitive intrusions into local affairs, but as necessary machinery in the direction and exercise of which the community must participate. The community of the realm of the thirteenth century had its roots deep in the social and tenurial structure of Anglo-Norman England.

17   FROM   *J. C. Holt*
                   Magna Carta, 1965

The following passage discusses the common elements in charters of liberties in western Europe.

Resistance to the abuse of monarchical power in the twelfth and thirteenth centuries was based on assumptions which permeated the society of western Europe. Magna Carta was more than a simple reaction against Angevin government, and more than a statement of the privileges which the Angevins had made available; it was also a statement of principles about the organization of a feudal state. As such it drew on a common body of experience and custom which, with local variants, was shared throughout western Europe and the Latin states in the east. Hence the Norman and Angevin kings had to contend with men who shared strong views on the constitution of society, on title to feudal property, on the right to judgement and on the proper conduct of lords and kings. The Angevins gave their men

SOURCE. J. C. Holt, *Magna Carta*, Cambridge University Press, 1965, pp. 63–68. Reprinted by permission of Cambridge University Press.

the grievances and the education in government which were woven into the tapestry of Magna Carta. But the warp and weft were derived from the structure of society itself.

This common experience was embodied in custumals and law-books, it was formulated in statutes, it was sharpened by the conflict between Church and State, it was laid down as assizes when new states were founded, and it was stated in charters of liberties when the interaction of royal policy and aristocratic interests exploded into political crises. Together these scattered and widely different sources reveal legal and political principles of remarkable permanence and pervasiveness. For example, the insistence on judgement by peers in cap. 39 of Magna Carta was simply an assertion of a generally recognized axiom. It received its first clear statement in the edict of the Emperor Conrad II of 1037 which laid down that military tenants were not to be de-prived of their fiefs "except by the laws of our ancestors and the judgement of their peers." In Italy it was repeated in the Treaty of Constance of 1183 and the concessions of Charles of Salerno of 1283. It was accepted procedure in actions between king and barons in the kingdom of Jerusalem. In France it cropped up in a wide variety of sources, in custumals and reports of actions in royal and honorial courts. In Normandy, it was bluntly stated in the Ancient Custumal of c. 1200 in the form—"peer ought to be judged by peer." In England the same principle was asserted in the Laws of Henry I in the form—"each man is to be judged by his peers of the same neighbourhood." It was assumed in the organization of the great honours in the early twelfth century and a man might still call upon his peers to substantiate his case in the royal courts at the end of the century.

This principle or method of judicial procedure owed its per-vasiveness to the general assumption in feudal societies that a lord was bound to do justice to his men and that vassals were bound to attend and constitute their lord's court. It also survived simply because it was a principle, a generalization open to inter-pretation, special construction and evasion. Yet it is only one example of many common principles, some of which were much more precise and categorical. For example, the feudal aristocracy reacted with astonishing single-mindedness throughout western Europe against demands for military service outside the realm. In England, Magna Carta contained no provision specifically on this point, but the burden of such service had contributed largely to the outbreak of rebellion and a demand for its limitation was initially included in the baronial programme. On the continent there was a widespread demand for the limitation or control of such service. In his statutes of 1188 Alphonso of Leon agreed that he would not make war or peace except by the advice of the bishops and nobles of the realm. In Aragon in 1283 Peter III agreed that he would only make war by the advice of nobles, knights and townsfolk and that the nobles were not bound by the conditions of their feudal tenures to serve overseas. In the Latin kingdom in the east it was recognized that the king could only ask for service outside its frontiers if it was to the general profit of the realm and even then the service was to be at the king's expense. In Hungary the Golden Bull of 1222 included the provisions that only the counts, and knights who were serving for pay, were bound to give service outside the realm. In France, the Statute of Pamiers of 1212, which established the customs of the new crusading state created by Simon de Montfort and his associates in Provence, laid down that the Count was not entitled to service except by grace and at his own pay if he wilfully intervened in wars which were irrelevant to the safety of himself or his country. Such views died hard. More than a century later the nobles and knights of Champagne asserted that any summons to military service should be made within the county and that they should not be required to serve outside the bounds of the county except at the king's own expense. In both these French examples the argument that military service should be local was closely similar to that which the northern opponents of King John advanced in 1213–15.

Military service created widespread and perennial acrimony. The problem of enforcing some real control over capricious kings was less enduring, yet even here the radical provisions of cap. 61 of Magna Carta had parallels elsewhere. In the kingdom of Jerusalem it was recognized that the king's vassals might resort to the renunciation of fealty and rebellion in certain specified circumstances, as, for example, when the king imprisoned or deprived a vassal without judgement or persistently denied justice to his men. In Hungary King Andrew II agreed in the Bull of 1222 that "if we or any of our successors ever wish to revoke this concession in any way, bishops, lords and nobles, each and every one, both now and in the future have our authority to resist and contradict us and our successors without taint of any infidelity." In Aragon, in the *Privilegio de la Union* of 1287, King Alphonso III pledged the good behaviour of the Crown by the surrender of sixteen castles and the acknowledgement that his vassals could choose another king if he contravened their privileges; in surrendering castles he provided a guarantee which had also been considered in England in 1215 in an unofficial version of Magna Carta which survived at St Albans. Even the papacy was affected by this kind of constitutional thinking. When Urban IV arranged to transfer the kingdom of Sicily to Charles of Anjou in 1263 he laid down that Charles was to force his new subjects to swear that they would transfer their fealty to the pope if he or his successors departed in any way from the conditions under which the pope was investing him with the kingdom. Urban optimistically ordered that the oath should be renewed every ten years in perpetuity. In the light of this it would perhaps be hasty to condemn the security clause of Magna Carta as unrealistic.

Liberties throughout western Europe embodied constantly recurring privileges. They asserted the property rights of the king's vassals and the limitation of the Crown's feudal prerogative; they insisted on lawful process against arbitrary action by the king or his ministers, and maintained that judges and administrators should be native born or local men; they insisted on the maintenance of ancient right and custom and the repeal of new impositions whether fiscal, administrative or jurisdictional. They relied on the same forms of security. Just as King John swore to observe the terms of the Great Charter in 1215, so Simon de Montfort swore to observe and maintain the Statute of Pamiers in 1212, Andrew II of Hungary the Golden Bull in 1231 and Alphonso III of Aragon the *Privilegio de la Union* of 1287. These liberties were cognate. There is no need to explain the many similarities between them as derivatives from some basic grant or legal code. There is no sound reason, for example, for believing that the Golden Bull owed anything to Magna Carta or that either of them owed anything directly to the assizes of the kingdom of Jerusalem or the Statute of Pamiers. Nowhere in there the exact verbal identity to establish such a link. Nowhere was there an exact identity of situation. Men from many different countries met and talked on pilgrimages, diplomatic missions and on the crusade. But they had no need to borrow constitutional solutions and legal principles from each other. In their home-lands they faced similar developments in monarchical power. They called on similar deep-rooted and unquestioned assump-tions about feudal rights and legal process. They turned to the same system of securities which depended on oaths, pledges, guarantees and guarantors, and they naturally provided similar political and legal solutions to keep royal power in check. The liberties of the twelfth and thirteenth centuries were no infection spreading from one country to another; they were part of the very atmosphere.

18   FROM   *J. C. Holt*
                Magna Carta, 1965

Myth has played a large part in the history of charters of liberties. The following passage demonstrates that myth and historical fiction were not simply subsequent accretions but com-ponent elements of the charters and the intellectual movement that produced them.

The first hesitant steps in these directions were pure fiction. Men convinced themselves that their present circumstances could be compared with an ideal past which had been governed by good and ancient laws. They therefore demanded the restoration of the Laws of Edward the Confessor and Henry I as the basic condition of reform, and they dragged out the charter of Henry I from the forgotten recesses of monastic and cathedral repositories and insisted on its confirmation. In some respects this appeal to tradition is readily comprehensible. The history of the Normans in England formed a unity stretching back to 1066 which could

SOURCE. J. C. Holt, *Magna Carta*, Cambridge University Press, 1965, pp. 96–98. Reprinted by permission of Cambridge University Press.

easily be grasped. Men were used to claiming title "from the conquest" even though tenure at the death of Henry I or the coronation of Henry II was all that was required in law. Moreover the coronation charters of the various kings traced custom and law back from 1154 to the reigns of Henry I and William I and so to the old English monarchy. In 1161 the penultimate English king, Edward the Confessor, had been canonized. In the late twelfth century his sanctity was known to include the remission of taxes. Hence Edward's memory was potent reinforcement for those who favoured governmental moderation. Even the papal legate, arguing his master's case before King John during the Interdict, could contrast the good customs of the holy Edward with the evil laws introduced by William the Bastard.

However, this appeal to tradition cannot be attributed entirely to the circumstances of the Norman Conquest, for it was also widespread on the continent. In the Golden Bull Andrew II of Hungary confirmed the privileges which his men had held in the time of St Stephen. In France, in 1314, Philip the Fair confirmed the liberties which his subjects had held under St Louis, and a year later Louis X had to acknowledge claims that evil customs had grown up since the time of the blessed Louis. In the kingdom of Sicily, where no member of the ruling family had achieved canonization, men had to make do with the memory of good King William II as a suitable standard to which Pope Urban required the Angevins to conform in 1263, and which they promised to accept when the events of 1282-3 forced reform upon them. Much of this had a clear political purpose. The men of Amiénois dragged St Louis in to cover demands which included private warfare. The nobles of Burgundy also appealed to his reign as if it established a standard of aristocratic privilege. In Sicily the reign of William the Good was used as a basis for reduced taxation. Everywhere these venerable monarchs were being used to resist and restrain the intrusions of their successors into the liberties of their subjects.

In some countries kings helped to bring this retribution upon their own heads, for they too had appealed to tradition to establish or recover royal rights. In Sicily the appeal to William the Good was first made by the Emperor Frederick II in an effort to recover rights of the Crown which had been lost during his own stormy minority. Likewise in England Henry II was responsible for the search for precedents in the reign of Henry I, for he deliberately set out to re-establish the Crown as it had been on the day his grandfather died. Hence for example he confirmed to the citizens of Exeter "all the rightful customs which they had in the time of King Henry my grandfather, revoking all evil customs which have arisen there since his day." Hence, too, the royal courts steadily rejected claims to property based on possession in the reign of Stephen. Henry II himself had helped to create the tradition which was to be used against his sons.

19 FROM   *The Golden Bull of*
                   Hungary, 1222, 1231

The Golden Bull, so called because it carried a gold seal, was first granted by King Andrew II in 1222 and again in amended form in 1231. The crisis that produced it arose partly from Andrew's costly involvement in the Crusade of 1217 and partly from the increasingly secure establishment of the Hungarian nobility which the bull acknowledged and confirmed. The texts are derived from confirmations of 1318 and 1351. The security clause of 1222 was replaced by a weakened version in 1231; both texts of this are given below. In 1351 cap. 4 was omitted and the security clause of 1222 was restored; it remained in the bull in all subsequent confirmations down to 1687 when it was finally rescinded. With that amendment the bull figured as an integral part of the coronation oath down to the end of the Hungarian monarchy.

CAP. 2. We also wish that neither we nor our successors shall ever seize or bring to ruin any of our tenants-in-chief[1] for the

[1] The translation of the Hungarian charters raises difficulties. I have translated *serviens* throughout as "tenant-in-chief." It has the sense, not of "sergeant" still less of "servant" but of one who owes service to the King.

SOURCE. H. Marczali, *Enchiridion Fontium Historiae Hungarorum*, Budapest 1901, pp. 134–143.

favour of some powerful person, unless he has first been summoned and convicted by judicial procedure.

CAP. 3. We shall allow no tax or levy of money to be made on the estates of our tenants-in-chief, nor shall we descend on houses or villages, unless invited, nor shall we levy taxes on the tenants of the Church.

CAP. 4. If any tenant-in-chief dies leaving no son, his daughter shall have a quarter of his possessions; he may dispose of the remainder as he wishes. And if death prevents him from making such disposition, his nearest relations shall have them; and if he has no relations at all the King shall have them.

CAP. 7. And if the King wishes to lead an army outside the realm tenants-in-chief are not bound to accompany him, except at his expense. . . If on the other hand an army comes against the realm all are bound to go together against it. If we wish to take an army outside the realm and we go with it, all those who have counties are bound to go with us, but at our expense.

CAP. 11. If foreigners who enjoy the king's protection come to the realm they shall not be promoted to dignities except by the counsel of the realm.

CAP. 13. The greater lords[2] as they follow the court or wherever they set forth, shall not oppress or despoil the poor.

CAP. 14. If any count does not conduct his office honestly or brings ruin to the people of his town and is convicted of this, let him be dishonourably deprived of his office before the witness of the whole realm and restore what he has taken.

CAP. 17. No one at any time shall be deprived of his possessions which he has obtained by lawful service.

CAP. 31. And so that this grant and ordinance should be valid both in our time and our successors', we have had it drawn up in seven copies and corroborated it with our gold seal. One copy shall be sent to the Lord Pope so that he may have it written in his register; the second is for the Hospital, the third for the Temple, the fourth shall remain with the King, the fifth shall go to the Chapter of Esztergom, the sixth to the Chapter of Kalocsa, and the seventh shall remain with the Count Palatine whoever may hold the office, so that he shall always have this writing before his eyes and shall never deviate in any way from

2 I have rendered *jobagio* throughout as "greater lord." In some chapters of the bull they are contrasted with the *servientes*.

the aforesaid, nor agree to the King or the nobles or any other so deviating; so that they shall enjoy their liberty and on that account show themselves faithful to us and our successors always and not deny the service due to the royal Crown.

And if we, or any of our successors, ever wish to revoke this concession in any way, then, by the authority of these letters, bishops, greater lords and nobles[3] of the realm, each and every one, both now and in the future shall have the right to resist and contradict us and our successors in perpetuity, without taint of any infidelity.

[In 1231 cap. 31 of the 1222 version was replaced by the following]

CAP. 36. So that these matters shall remain firm and unbroken both in our time and our successors', both we and our sons have confirmed them by corporal oath, and we have caused them to be corroborated with both our own and our sons' seals. And we willingly agree that if either we or our sons or our successors wish to break the liberty which has been granted, then the Archbishop of Esztergom, after lawful warning, shall have the power of placing us under the bond of excommunication.

20　　FROM　　　　*The Charter of the
Normans 1315*

The French charters of 1315–1316 were issued in response to the demands of the various Leagues of the Nobility which had been founded in 1314–1315. These leagues marked the culmination of opposition to the financial and administrative consequences of the costly interventions of Philip IV (1285–1314) in the Mediterranean, against Aragon, in Flanders, and against England. There were also strong objections to currency manipulation by the Crown; see caps. 1 and 2 below. The French Leagues

───────────────

3 "Nobles" is simply a translation of *nobilis*.

SOURCE. *Ordonnances des Roys de France de la Troisième Race*, vol. 1, ed. E. de Laurière, Paris 1723, pp. 587–594.

*were provincial; although they cooperated occasionally, their
demands were met by provincial charters which tended to confirm or restate provincial privilege. Charters of this kind were
granted to Normandy, Languedoc, Brittany, Burgundy, Picardie,
Champagne, Auvergne, Basses Marches (the old lands of the
Angevin house: Poitou, Touraine, Anjou, Maine, Saintonge,
Angoumois), Berry, and Nivernais. Of these the Breton charter
was confirmed in 1324; the charters to Languedoc, in 1328, 1368,
1446 and 1463; and the Charter to the Normans in 1339 (by
John, Duke of Normandy, eldest son of Philip VI), 1380, 1423
(by John, Duke of Bedford, regent of France during the English
occupation), 1458, and 1462. The charter was also registered at
the Parlement of Paris in 1381 and enrolled at the Exchequer
of Rouen in 1462. It was issued in two versions in March 1315,
and one or other of these was incorporated in many texts of the*
Custumal of Normandy.[1] *Extracts are given below from the
second and longer version.*

Louis, by the grace of God, King of the French, to all our
faithful men and justices, greeting and peace. We have received
a serious complaint from prelates, churchmen, knights and other
nobles, subjects and commons of the Duchy of Normandy, alleging that since the time of St. Louis, our great-grandfather
many burdens and novelties have been imposed on them: *tailles,*
taxes and divers impositions contrary to the usual custom of the
land and its rights and liberties; from which grave scandals are
threatened and endless prejudice is created against them and
their heirs and successors. Wherefore they have humbly besought
us that we should deign to provide a suitable remedy for the
aforesaid complaints which they have most earnestly placed
before us. And indeed, being favourably inclined to their prayers
. . . after solemn deliberation with our counsel on these requests,
we have determined to provide and ordain:—

---

[1] A. Artonne, *Le Mouvement de 1314 et les chartes provinciales de 1315,*
Paris, 1912, especially pp. 147–162 from which the above information is
taken.

CAP. 1. We concede, determine and ordain for them and their heirs and successors, that henceforth in the said Duchy of Normandy, neither we nor our successor will cause there to be any currency other than the *tournois,* the *parisis* and the great *tournois,* and coins of white metal of the weight and value they had in the time of my great-grandfather, nor shall we allow any other money to be current in any way, especially since, to this end, we receive from long past fixed renders every three years in the said Duchy.

CAP. 2. That we shall not arrange to levy the renders due to us for not changing the said money, which in the said Duchy are called *moneyage* or *fouage,*[2] nor allow them to be levied in any way, except as contained in the register of the custom of Normandy, any contrary practice in the aforesaid notwithstanding.

CAP. 3. Those men, both noble and non-noble, who owe fixed services to us and our successors in wartime and in our armies, shall remain free and immune once those services have been performed, nor can they be compelled by us or our successors to perform further service against their will except in a case where for some urgent reason, . . . the *arrière-ban* is appropriate.

CAP. 4. When the men of our aforesaid Duchy have performed their service due to us either in our army or in some other way, we neither can nor ought to claim or pretend in any way to the services and aids due from their subtenants, saving our right in the case of *arrière-ban.*

CAP. 7. Neither we nor our successors can or ought to claim from either persons or goods within the said Duchy any tallage, tax, imposition or exaction or whatever kind, other than the revenues, customary payments and services due to us, unless evident and urgent necessity demands it.

CAP. 14. That every noble, or any other man by reason of the dignity of his fief which he holds in the Duchy of Normandy, shall henceforth have complete right to take wreck and stray in his land, as is contained in the register of the custom of Normandy, notwithstanding any usage to the contrary.

CAP. 15. That henceforth we and our successors are bound to

---

2 *fouage, focagium*: so called because the levy was assessed on the hearth, *focus.*

send sufficient and suitable Inquisitors[3] throughout our Duchy of Normandy every three years in order to reform, correct and punish the excesses of any of our officials who hold office in the aforesaid Duchy.

Cap. 16. That henceforth in the Duchy of Normandy no free man shall be put to interrogation or torture unless strong presumption and certain conjecture render him suspect of a capital crime, and in such a case, in which he ought to be put to torture, he shall be subjected to it in such a way and with such moderation that neither death nor mutilation of the limbs are incurred because of the severity of the torture.

Cap. 18. Since the pleas of the Duchy of Normandy ought to be settled by local custom they shall henceforth be terminated or determined by sentence, in the Exchequer of Rouen, and henceforth they shall in no wise be brought, by whatever route, either to us or our Parlement of Paris; neither can anyone be adjourned to our Parlement in the pleas of the aforesaid Duchy.

Cap. 19. That henceforth in the Duchy of Normandy forty years' prescription shall suffice as effective title, whether the point at issue concerns the whole of high or ordinary justice or any matter pertaining thereto, or any other kind of business. And if anyone in the Duchy of Normandy, of whatever condition or state he may be, has had peaceful possession of the aforesaid or any part of the aforesaid [rights of jurisdiction] for forty years, he shall suffer no further interference in the matter, nor will our justices permit any interference to occur. . .

---

[3] This chapter represents an attempt to revive procedures instituted by Louis IX in 1247.

21   FROM   *R. Altamira*
          Magna Carta and Spanish Medieval
                    Jurisprudence

The great Spanish jurist and historian, Rafael Altamira, 1866–
1951, judge of the permanent court of International Justice, wrote
this essay as a contribution to the commemoration of the 700th
anniversary of Magna Carta. The second part of the essay, in
which he is concerned with sanctions on the Crown, is reproduced
below. Further comparisons with Spanish liberties are made in
nos. 16, 17, and 23.

Let us now pass to the most important point of comparison
between Magna Carta and Spanish Jurisprudence in the thirteenth century, the point which most clearly marks the tendency
of political evolution in Europe and which, for that reason,
produced most results in the direction of constitutional control.
That point is the attitude of the barons towards the despotism
of John Lackland and the guarantees with which they surrounded
the concessions obtained, lest the King should evade those concessions. In fact, the whole scheme of declarations and promises
contained in Magna Carta is valueless apart from security for
their accomplishment. Many Spanish kings made identical or
similar promises, and the same thing occurred in other European
countries which were passing through the same movement. But
the real practical problem does not lie in declarations on the
part of one section of the community, or of several sections, or
of the whole people (whether represented in Cortes or not) that
they propose to limit and censure the King's exercise of authority. The point is the possession of power to accomplish that
object. One method of doing this was to bind the King with a
series of guarantees constituting for him a danger or a con-

SOURCE. R. Altamira, "Magna Carta and Spanish Medieval Jurisprudence,"
Magna Carta Commemoration Essays, ed. E. H. Malden, Royal Historical Society, London 1917, pp. 237–243. Reprinted by permission of the Council of
the Royal Historical Society.

siderable difficulty in the ordinary working of his authority and his administration.

In Spain, from the Visigothic period onwards, efforts are clearly visible to check the natural propensity of kings towards abuse of power—a propensity which is found in all authority. But the means chosen are either merely moral definitions—such as maxims declaring the King to be the first subject of the laws— or else legal declarations of guarantees which rest solely on the monarch's good faith, such as limitations of the confiscation of private property. The sole effective counterpoise lies in the King's perpetual apprehension about breaking his formal and legal undertakings, in view of the powerful forces concerned in their enforcement. At a later time, the Cortes constitute a sys- tematized guarantee by means of which the people hold the King in subjection through the power of refusing what the King may require, that is to say supplies; but in all other respects, equi- librium—which was seldom really secured—is produced or at- tempted through the free play of the two counterbalancing forces. And this is why in Castile the power of the municipalities and the whole body of privileges represented by the municipal "fueros"[1] are so valuable, while in Aragon the social weight of the nobility possesses a similar value.

Magna Carta treats the question in quite another manner. The creation of the committee of twenty-five barons (ch. 61) as a kind of tribunal to judge infringements of privilege and the functions assigned to this committee in chapters 52 and 55, as well as the recognition of the right of insurrection in case of breach of faith on the King's part, constitute guarantees which already assume an almost constitutional form.

Both these provisions are known to Spanish jurisprudence, but they only attain a similar constitutional force considerably later than the date of Magna Carta. The first device, that of the committee of barons, as a tribunal to watch over the fulfilment of the "peace and liberties" granted and confirmed in the Char- ter, in Aragon takes the form of the "Justicia Mayor," in so far as that dignitary, forced upon the King by the nobles, becomes mediating judge or judge of "contrafuero," that is to say, ex- aminer of infringements of law committed by the King or his

---

[1] *Fueras*: liberties, privileges, as embodied in charter or statute.

officials. This guarantee was initiated in the Cortes of Egea in 1265. Its complete development is found in the "Privilegio General" won from Pedro III in 1283 and is still more marked in the "Privilegio de la Unión" (1287) which forbade the King to take proceedings against any adherent of the Union, whether nobleman or municipality, without the intervention of a judicial sentence by the "Justicia" and the consent of the Cortes. Something in the same direction, but less effective, is to be found in the privilege of the Aragonese and also the Catalonian Cortes that examination should first be made of any grievances against the King.

In Castile there was nothing resembling the committee of twenty-five barons before the Pact ("pacto") of the Hermandad[2] of the nobles and municipalities ("concejos") of Castile, León, and Galicia with the infante Don Sancho, son of Alfonso X (1282). This Pact established the right of the Hermandad to judge the royal officials and even the judges themselves and to inflict upon them punishments, including the penalty of death. This privilege or means of security against the King and his officials finds its culmination in the "Concordia de Medina," which was forced upon Henry IV in 1463: but this latter agreement was short-lived.

The second device, that of insurrection, is more fully represented in Castile. The earliest document which we know concerning this is the above-mentioned Pact of 1282, which assigns to the towns the right of insurrection against royal infringements of the law. The same thing occurs in what may be called political programmes of other Hermandades of the thirteenth century, such as the Hermandades which united the towns of Castile, León, and Galicia in 1295, and which were confirmed by Ferdinand IV. A similar provision is found in the above-mentioned "Concordia de Medina," which establishes the right of making war on the King without incurring penalty, in case the King should proceed against nobles or ecclesiastics in any other form than that formulated in that document. It would be out of place here to discuss the doctrinal development of this right of insurrection in the hands of theologians and political theorists of the

2 *Hermandad*: association, confraternity.

sixteenth and seventeenth centuries: this important topic has given rise to an abundant critical literature in recent times.

In Aragon, assertions of the right of insurrection were at least as definite as in Castile, and had wider results in the sequence of political events. The "Privilegio de la Unión" declared that, in case the King infringed its provisions, the leagued nobles and municipalities were free to refuse him obedience and choose another sovereign without being guilty of treason. Notwithstanding the astute government of James II, this privilege was ratified in 1347, when the new King, Pedro IV, was obliged to recognize the power, claimed by the Union, of deposing, banishing, and depriving the King, if he should inflict punishment without the judicial sentence of the "Justicia" and the advice of the "ricos-hombres." But this "Privilegio" was not valid for long in Aragon, since Pedro IV himself annulled it in 1348.

To conclude, it is interesting to compare the very wide character of these securities—that of insurrection and that of a tribunal or judge to examine royal infringements of law—in most of the Castilian and Aragonese documents concerning them, with the very special and limited character which they bear in Magna Carta. The competence of the tribunal of twenty-five barons and the right of insurrection refer explicitly to the "peace and liberties" granted and defined in Magna Carta, whereas the similar securities embodied in contemporary or slightly later Spanish jurisprudence embrace every possible case of infringement of privilege on the part of the King or of his officials, although these documents sometimes particularly mention irregularities of legal procedure. The greater amplitude which in Spain from the beginning marks the guarantees won by nobles and by the people, may arise either from a natural propensity of the Spanish mind to generalize without giving much importance to the generalization, or else from a complete view of the problem and a desire to solve it entirely once for all. Whichever be the explanation, it is a characteristic trait of our history.

Another characteristic is the constant mixture of noble and of popular elements in these acts of resistance to royal despotism and to arbitrary administration. The joint action of both classes signifies that in Spain the liberties obtained had a very wide social reach, especially in Castile, where popular action had a large share in the movement. But it should not be forgotten that in many cases—especially in Aragon, but also in Castile during the reign of Henry IV—the pressure put upon the King had an oligarchical character, a condition of things which is in fact not less dangerous than royal despotism to public rights. The conflict arises, not always between a despot and a people suffering under his despotism, but sometimes between a despot and other despots who resist a check upon their despotism. That is to say, class privileges are asserted against the authority of one man's will; and this fact should be well weighed—as it has been weighed by modern writers on Magna Carta—in order not to attribute to political development a much more democratic tendency than it really possessed. What did happen was that those who strove to limit the royal will in their own interests were unwittingly furthering constitutional progress on behalf of all. For they were preparing both the minds of men and the machinery of government in such a way that, when the royal power, representing the unity of the State, should rise above the diversity of aristocratic and local authorities, this single power should not be in a position to injure the fundamental rights of the subject.

The dates at which this point was reached and the roads which led to its attainment have varied in all the countries of Europe. Every country has also differed from its neighbours in the vicissitudes of advance and retrogression. In England, apart from some episodes of fluctuating movement, the tendency of national liberties becomes continually more marked from 1215, and soon takes a decisive and progressive direction. In Spain, notwithstanding her priority in this kind of political activity, privileges are lost without any compensating gain to the common rights of subjects; for the absolute power of the King dominates all privileges, and destroys that which had been attained in the Middle Ages; nor is the loss replaced by any analogous guarantees of equal extent. The process is interrupted and is renewed long afterwards, in the nineteenth century, without the attainment of positive advantages until near the end of that century. But the true history of absolute power in Spain, in order to elucidate how far it penetrated civil and political jurisprudence, still remains to be studied; and any generalization would be, at the present time, premature.

22   FROM   *Antonio Marongiu*
     The Contractual Nature of Parliamentary
                   Agreements

Antonio Marongiu, Professor of the History of Law in the University of Rome, here discusses the relationship between charters of liberties and the medieval parliaments and estates. He argues that they supported each other and hence shared a common fate at the hands of the absolute monarchies which were established from the sixteenth century.

We have seen how in their origins parliamentary institutions were strengthened by the diffusion of the democratic concept implicit in the formula *quod omnes tangit*.[1] Similarly, in the age of absolutism the assemblies found the strength to survive through the deep-rooted belief in the contractual nature of agreements between sovereigns and their peoples or estates.

Medieval history is marked by solemn agreements or constitutions accepted by sovereigns in response to demands that rights be recognised. These demands were made by subjects who claimed special recognition because of their legal status or political actions. A well-known series of such agreements can be pointed to in the 12th, 13th and 14th centuries: the peace of Constance of 1183, Alfonso IX's constitution for León of 1188, the Magna Carta of 1215, the Golden Bull of Hungary of 1222, the Provisions of Oxford of 1258, the *privilegio general* of Aragon of 1283, the Castilian constitution of Valladolid of 1307, the *Joyeuse*

---

[1] *quod omnes tangit [ab omnibus approbetur]*; "what touches all is to be approved by all"; derived from Roman and Canon Law, this maxim was used frequently as explanatory jargon for parliamentary and consultative institutions in both ecclesiastical and secular administration.

SOURCE. A. Marongiu, trans. S. J. Woolf, *Medieval Parliaments*, London 1968, pp. 233–235. Reprinted by permission of Casa Editrice. Dott A. Giuffrè.

entrée[2] of Brabant of 1356. But there is also an even longer series of agreements whose contractual nature is masked by their formal description as unilateral "gracious" concessions: for example, the oath of Jean de Valenrode of Liége of 1418, the agreement of 1472 between the marquis and estates of Brandenburg, the pact of Tübingen of 1514. The purpose of each of these constitutional agreements was to settle ideological or political conflicts, and to establish or register a new equilibrium of forces. Each intended to delimit the extent of the sovereign's powers in relation to the rights he recognised as belonging to the people. The agreements were often broken by the ruler, but even this did not imply a repudiation of the principle and practice of collaboration, or of the agreements and pacts between sovereign and people.

The importance of these agreements was underlined by their insistence upon the perpetuity and irrevocability of the concessions, and by their acceptance by the sovereigns as contracts between two parties. They reflected the limited nature of sovereignty in the Middle Ages.

The sovereign needed the collaboration of his subjects, and hence had to reach agreement with them through reciprocal concessions. He took the initiative by summoning his subjects to an assembly to ask for their advice and aid. The agreements reached in these assemblies marked the boundary between his power and the original rights or acquired privileges of the people—or rather of the estates or communities—who thus gained acknowledged powers within the state.

Nor were these pacts purely theoretical. A regular and continuous series of agreements were made in parliament which required application. The parliaments, estates or *bracci* discussed and decided upon the demands of the government, just as sovereigns and governments examined, modified and accepted parliamentary requests. All these agreements were bilateral contracts, but they applied to the administrative system. Thus, on both the political and administrative level, relations between sovereign and country were based on contractual assumptions.

2 *Joyeuse entrée*; charter granted by Wenceslas of Luxembourg on his recognition as Duke of Brabant and entry into the title and Duchy; also used for other charters granted in similar circumstances in the Low Countries. See Suggestions for Further Reading, below pp. 189–90.

With the development of absolutism from the 15th century, not only were parliamentary institutions and all surviving forms of corporative or territorial autonomies attacked, but so also were contractualist concepts. Ferdinand the Catholic denied all affirmations of bilateral obligations in Sicily; Charles V and Emanuel Philibert of Savoy refused to swear the traditional oaths to observe the concessions of their predecessors; the Spanish court no longer wanted to hear of "donatives," with their implication of a voluntary act, but insisted instead upon "services."

As the polemic between the surviving assemblies and the supporters of absolutism developed, the question whether or not sovereigns were bound to observe inviolably the contracts they had agreed with their subjects acquired a special interest. Could the king impose taxation and lay down laws without the consent of his subjects? If the king had made some agreement, was it perpetually valid, even if the sovereign maintained that it was prejudicial to his prerogatives and the good of the country? It is in 16th-century France that the discussion can be followed most easily, in the writings of Hotman, Matharel, Bodin and Grégoire; for where sovereigns attempted to assert their absolute power, the polemic became most lively. But not only in France but in Catalonia, Aragon, Sicily and Sardinia, the parliamentarian doctrine was asserted both in publicists' writings and in parliamentary discussions and declarations. In 15th-century Catalonia, Tomas Mieres asserted that it was clear that royal constitutions, once sworn by the sovereign, were of perpetual validity and could not be derogated or revoked by the sovereign, while contrary acts could have no validity, even if reinforced by further oaths. In the 1660s the advocate of the military *stament* of Sardinia, D. Joseph Martinez Figueras Alarcon, sent a memorial to Queen Maria Teresa of Spain asserting the perpetual validity of old agreements. On the opposing side, the chanceries claimed unconditional obedience, and were supported by other publicists.

The survival of parliamentary doctrines in this rising tide of absolutism was assisted, at least in part, by the widespread publication of the old texts: for these laws underlined the reciprocal nature of the concessions and so justified the defence of ancient privileges granted "with the force of contracts," or "as perpetual privileges" or as "laws agreed by pact."

But in the 17th and 18th centuries, as the tradition grew

weaker, it became more difficult to assert the contractualist concept with confidence. As policies of enlightened despotism were imposed, the position of the parliaments was further weakened by the claim of the sovereigns to work directly for the public interest, without the representative bodies acting as intermediaries.

23   FROM   *J. C. Holt*
Magna Carta, 1965

The following passage discusses some of the contrasts between Magna Carta and other medieval liberties.

The Great Charter was a grant to "all free men of our realm." It presupposed a wide market for its benefactions. It was not unique in this. The ordinances of Leon of 1188 were issued in favour of "all of my realm, clerical and lay" and they were drawn up in a session of the king's court which included citizens and knights as well as magnates and bishops. The Golden Bull of Hungary of 1222 was conceded to "nobles and other men of the realm." In Aragon the *Privilegio General* of 1283 was granted to "great men, mesne tenants, knights, nobles, citizens and all and every man in our realm." In Sicily one of the conditions which Urban IV laid down for Charles of Anjou was that he should maintain the privileges of "counts, barons, knights and all men in his realm." Perhaps on the continent there was a more obvious tendency to enumerate the various social grades on which privileges were conferred, but this in itself is scarcely significant. The Magna Carta of 1225 was granted not to "all free men of our realm" as in 1215 but to "archbishops, bishops, abbots, priors, earls, barons, and all of our realm." With this list few continental grants could compete.

SOURCE. J. C. Holt, *Magna Carta,* Cambridge University Press, 1965, pp. 180–185. Reprinted by permission of Cambridge University Press.

Some of the continental liberties, however, were much more restricted than these. The concessions made at Constance in 1183 were concerned exclusively with the privileges of the towns of the Lombard League. Frederick II's concessions of 1220 were addressed to the ecclesiastical princes of the Empire as were those of 1231–2 to the secular princes and magnates. A narrow base for privilege was again revealed in the Sicilian concessions of 1283 which were made to "barons, counts and other holders of fiefs." It was illustrated finally, and perhaps most clearly of all, in the various petitions, ordinances, and charters produced in France during the crisis of 1314–15. These occasionally suggest that the demands made against the king were widely based. The resistance to the Crown in Picardy, Artois, Beauvaisis, Vermandois and Ponthieu came from a league of the nobility and lesser men. In Burgundy the league included the representatives from eleven towns. In Normandy Louis X recorded that there had been complaints from "prelates, churchmen, knights, other nobles and subjects and commons." But such evidence is rare and meant very little. Most of the documents of these quarrels told a different story. In 1314 Philip the Fair's concessions were made "at the instance of barons and nobles of the realm of France, leagued together to recover the privileges, liberties, franchises, customs and immunities enjoyed by churchmen, dukes, counts and other subjects of the King of the French in the time of St Louis." In Normandy Louis X negotiated with the "barons, knights and other noble subjects and bishops," in Burgundy with the "nobles" or "the clergy and nobles," in Amiénois with the "nobles" and in Champagne with the "nobles and other persons."

Throughout Europe the sharp aristocratic flavour of these documents fairly represented their real content. In the kingdom of Sicily the concessions of 1283 paid some attention to the great towns of southern Italy, but it was in the main concerned with aristocratic privilege. It laid down for example that "no services were to be demanded from counts, barons and other noble and knightly men, which did not become their estate and condition." In Germany the concessions of 1220 and 1231 were aimed at securing princely privilege even to the damage of the towns which turned to seek imperial protection against aristocratic encroachment. In France the ordinance of 1314 and the provincial charters of 1315 were almost exclusively concerned with the

maintenance and revival of feudal jurisdiction, with the recovery
of the right of private war, with the exclusion of royal officials
from fiefs and with the exemption of the nobility from royal
jurisdiction. These were the foundation charters of a *noblesse*.
They promoted rather than healed class division. In 1316 Philip
V was able to persuade the nobles of Champagne to abandon
their conspiracy by arguing that aristocratic leagues excited the
lower orders. The leagues did in fact provoke isolated attacks
against seignorial jurisdiction. The contemporary song, the *Dit
des Alliés*, blamed the nobles for seeking their own selfish ends
and argued that justice was to be sought not at the hands of the
aristocracy but from the Crown. In some areas such charges were
justified. In Champagne the league was sustained by the personal
ambition of Louis de Nevers, in Picardy by the intervention of
Robert of Artois, who was pursuing a claim to the county, and
by the Count of Flanders. In Picardy the towns sided with the
Crown.

Magna Carta provoked nothing like the *Dit des Alliés*. This
was a fair reflexion of its quality. It was not alone in taking non-
baronial interests into account. Just as Magna Carta limited the
amercement of villeins so as not to deprive them of their livelihood and restricted the king's bailiffs' exercise of purveyance, so
the Golden Bull of Hungary provided that the king's ministers
as they followed the court or moved about the country were not
to oppress or despoil the poor, and that counts were to lose their
offices if they "destroyed" the people in their charge. But Magna
Carta acknowledged non-baronial interests far more than most
of the continental concessions and it covered a wider range of
such interests more thoroughly than any other similar grant.
This is partly revealed in the clauses concerned with municipal
privilege, with trade, and with the interests of freeholders. It is
demonstrated most convincingly of all in cap. 60 which laid
down that all the liberties which the king had conferred on his
men they in their turn would confer on their men. This was
not simply laid down as an airy principle. It was enforced precisely in cap. 15 of the Charter, which provided that the king
should not grant permission for anyone to take an aid from his
vassals except on the three occasions on which the Crown itself
might take a gracious aid. Similarly cap. 16, which laid down
that nobody was to be compelled to do more service than he

ought for his tenement, was equally applicable whether the lord was the king or a great baron. So also were the provisions on wardship, marriage and the rights of widows. When the framers of the Charter set out to protect the interests of under-tenants, they meant business. Within ten years knights and freeholders in Westmorland and Lancashire appealed to the principles of cap. 60 against the magnates of these counties and the Crown proceeded to order its enforcement.

This comprehensive quality of Magna Carta was revealed in many different ways. It was a grant to all free men throughout the realm. The French charters of 1315, in contrast, were provincial. Such inadequately consorted action as the French nobility managed to achieve was the result of treaties and alliance between one local league and another. Then again Magna Carta used the term "free man" in a characteristic and unique manner. The sense of these words varied. In cap. 15, which protected the free man from unreasonable demands for aids from his lord, the words clearly applied to under-tenants. This sense is also consistent with cap. 30, which protected the free man's horses and carts from seizure by the king's bailiffs. In cap. 34, in contrast, the Charter assumed that the "free man" might hold a court, the jurisdiction of which could be infringed by the writ *praecipe*. Such a court would enjoy much more than petty manorial jurisdiction. The drafters of the Charter also used these words comprehensively to describe the whole spectrum of social grades which held land by free tenure. Hence in cap. 27 they provided that where a "free man" died intestate his chattels were to be distributed by his nearest relatives and friends and by the view of the Church. Similarly the most famous of all the provisions of the Charter, cap. 39, erected defences against arbitrary imprisonment and disseisin by the king which it applied not to any one social grade or even to an enumeration of them, but to the free man. Most strikingly of all, cap. 9 of the Articles, which dealt with amercements, distinguished only three social grades —villeins, merchants and free men. These provisions were expanded in the Charter, which laid down that barons were to be amerced by their peers.[1] Until that exception was made it seems that they too were included in the general provision for free

[1] Cap. 21.

men. Even after they had been excepted the provision covering the amercement of free men still applied to all non-baronial tenants, and hence to military tenants holding their lands by knight service.

This broad generic use of the term "free man" is not matched in any other similar concession or statement of laws and liberties. It is most closely approached perhaps in cap. 28 of the Statute of Pamiers, which provided that "no man is to be sent to prison or held captive as long as he can give sufficient pledges of standing to right."[2] But there was no exact parallel even here, for the drafters of the statute clearly used the term "man" in contradistinction to the term "lord." Their thinking was far removed from that laid bare in Magna Carta. Other continental grants showed similar differences. The section in the Golden Bull of Hungary which most closely approached cap. 39 of Magna Carta laid down that "no noble was to be taken or destroyed for the favour of any powerful lord unless he had first been summoned and convicted by judicial process." Similarly the chapter of the Sicilian concessions of 1283 which provided for judgement by peers was restricted to "counts, barons and holders of fiefs."

Magna Carta then assumed legal parity among all free men to an exceptional degree. This automatic acceptance of a cohesive society had important results. The documents of 1215 assumed that the liberties at issue were to be held by a community, not by a series of individuals of this or that status, but by the realm.

2 For the Statute of Pamiers see above pp. 124–5.

PART FOUR

"Liberties" and "Liberty"

24 FROM *A. F. Pollard*
Parliament and Liberty

A. F. Pollard, Professor of Constitutional History, University College London, 1903–1931, founder and first director of the Institute of Historical Research 1920–1931, was probably the most influential of the many scholars who have drawn a sharp distinction between medieval "liberties" and modern "liberty." Pollard's work gave the argument wide currency. He also gave it a sharp and original flavor by maintaining that the two notions were not simply different but mutually inimical.

It has been remarked by a skilled American observer of English politics that "private property in England is, on the whole, less secure from attack on the part of the Government to-day than it was at the time of the Stuarts." A similar substratum of truth would underlie the statement that there was greater liberty before the beginning of parliaments than there has been since or is likely to be again; and the days when a wealthy magnate like Peter des Roches could evade a tax by voting against it must seem to many a golden age of liberty and property, from which England has been steadily falling away ever since parliaments

SOURCE. Alfred Frederick Pollard, *The Evolution of Parliament*, 2nd edition (London: Longmans, Green & Co., 1926; New York: Russell & Russell, 1964), pp. 166–177. Reprinted by permission of the publishers.

were invented to rob the individual of his liberty by means of
other men's votes. There is, however, no end to the paradoxes
for which liberty has been the excuse or the justification. The
crimes perpetrated in its name have been as multifarious as the
sins committed on behalf of religion or the battles fought for
the sake of peace.

It is the penalty of general and inspiring conceptions that they
mean so many different things and inspire different minds in so
many different ways. "When I mention religion," said the frank
but reverend M. Thwackum, "I mean the Christian religion; and
not only the Christian religion, but the Protestant religion; and
not only the Protestant religion, but the Church of England."
Orthodoxy is my 'doxy; heterodoxy is other people's. True liberty
is my liberty; other people's is their presumption. Servants take
liberties, but are not often, in the minds of their masters or their
mistresses, entitled to what they take. "Like every other struggle
for liberty," writes Bishop Stubbs of the Great Civil War, "it
ended in being a struggle for supremacy." Charles I fought for
liberty no less than did the parliament or the army, the English,
the Irish, or the Scots. Both north and south fought for liberty
in the American civil war, the north for the liberty of the negroes
in the south, the south for liberty to manage its own affairs.
Masters and men are fighting all over the world for liberty,
masters for liberty to employ their capital as they think fit, men
for liberty to choose their own conditions of labour. Like charity,
liberty covers a multitude of sins.

Nothing has proved more elusive than liberty, and its endless
pursuit has filled the pages of English history. Men thought, and
still think, it was achieved by Magna Carta; but it had to be
fought for again in the fourteenth century, in the Great Civil
War, and at the Revolution of 1688. Glorious as it seemed to
the Whigs, even that vindication of liberty failed to satisfy men
for long; reform bills in the nineteenth century were one after
another hailed as heralds of a newer freedom; and even after the
parliament act of 1911 liberty seems to some of us farther off
than ever. Nor are we singular in our discontents. The thirteen
American colonies fought a war of independence to achieve
their liberty: they won, but three-quarters of a century later
they were still fighting a sterner civil war for liberty; and the
latest generation of freeborn Americans carried into office and

power in 1912 a president whose banner bore the strange device "the new freedom." Man, said Rousseau, is born free, and everywhere he is in chains; man, it would rather seem, is born a slave and ever he is seeking to burst his bonds.

The fallacy lies in "man"; it also lies in "liberty." To say that man has achieved liberty is an inaccurate way of stating that some men have achieved some liberty. The problem of liberty, like that of property, is one of distribution, and cannot be divorced from that of equality. There was sense and logic in the union of the trinity of the French Revolution: there can be no liberty without some equality. But the third of the trio, fraternity, supplies—at least to an American student—the best illustration of the difficulty we have to face in tracing the growth of liberty. Every American undergraduate knows what a fraternity is; to an English undergraduate it looks like an embryo college. It is a voluntary association of students for social—some think for anti-social—purposes. Like every association, its value consists quite as much in the many undesirable persons it excludes as in the select few it comprehends. Fraternities are, indeed, too select for ultra-democratic feeling in the United States, and in more than one legislature bills have been introduced to abolish them as contraventions of democratic principle. Now, if a measure were passed by congress guaranteeing to all fraternities in perpetuity their privileges and their property, it is easily conceivable that such a measure might come to be called the great charter of fraternities. But it is not less easy to understand that the excluded majority might fail to discern any connexion between such a measure and the democratic ideal of fraternity.

That is the position of Magna Carta. It is the great charter of liberties, but not of liberty, and few habits are more fatal to historical understanding than that of assuming that the same word has the same meaning at different periods. We have no constants in history. It is far safer to assume discrepancy than identity, and it is an elementary precaution to warn beginners in history that medieval Germany might include Austria but not Prussia, Cambrai but not Breslau. These changes in the territorial meaning of familiar terms are comparatively simple and obvious; the vicissitudes in the terminology of ideas are more subtle, and even eminent archivists have provided striking illustrations of the dangers of ignoring them. Sir T. Duffus Hardy assumed that *religio* in the thirteenth century meant religion, and was astonished at John's modernism when he discovered a royal licence *condere novam religionem,* although John was guilty of nothing worse than granting a baron leave to found a religious house by alienating certain lands into mortmain. Yet the difference between *religio* and religion was not greater than that between *libertas* and liberty; and John was as medievally-minded when he granted Magna Carta as when he licensed a baron to found an abbey.

The medieval *libertas* and *religio* have this in common to distinguish them from their modern synonyms. Both were con-crete and material; both are now abstract and ideal. The trans-formation from the one to the other has been the common characteristic of linguistic development. The expansion of a nation's mind is seen, like that of a child's, in the expansion of the meaning attached to the terms it uses. One child has been known to think that Eleanor of Aquitaine was corpulent because she was described in a textbook as "one of Henry II's stoutest adherents"; and another imbibed the same idea of God from being told of His omnipresence. Liberty and religion are very local to primitive minds: local gods become tribal deities, and then the national gods of chosen peoples. But even Israel revolted against a God which had to be worshipped in Judah, as England murmured against a pope in Avignon, and nations had to ad-vance far on the path of civilization before they relinquished their conviction that their God spoke in their vernacular and gave them special protection in battle.

Their liberties were as their deities, peculiar to themselves, circumscribed in their operation, bound to the soil, tangible, visible, and concrete. The *genius loci* was at the bottom of both; and famous shrines had their counterpart in great liberties. The general idea was lost in the local manifestation; and our Lady of Walsingham belongs to the same class of phenomena as the "liberties of the Fleet." Liberties were always attached to particu-lar persons or places; there was nothing general or national about them. They were definite concrete privileges, which some people enjoyed, but most did not. The first clause of Magna Carta— "that the English church shall be free"—seems to be general enough; but the explanation that follows shows that all it meant was that cathedral chapters should be free to elect their bishops,

and presumably that the king should not be free to refuse them
their temporalities. Possibly the explanation was a royalist gloss,
and the demand for ecclesiastical freedom meant, in the minds
of those who made it, that the restrictions imposed on the liberties of the church by the Constitutions of Clarendon (1164)
should be ignored: as a matter of practice they were ignored in
the later middle ages, and this was assuredly a more general
liberty than any conceded in the charter. For the rest, the
liberties of "the church" were simply the sum of the particular liberties of each ecclesiastic. They were rights of patronage
and jurisdiction; and contention over these "liberties" of the
church is quite as rife in the middle ages among churchmen
themselves as between church and state. In both spheres alike
liberty was an adjunct, almost a form, of property; and it was
prized for its material and financial attributes.

It was almost always a local monopoly. The liberty of a town
consisted largely in its right to rate its inhabitants and to levy
tolls on all who frequented its markets. The liberty of a baron
consisted in his authority over others, in the court he owned,
and in the perquisites of his jurisdiction. To deprive him of this
jurisdiction over his villeins was an infringement of his liberty
expressly prohibited by the thirty-fourth clause of the charter.
Another infringement of liberty forbidden by the charter was
the reduction of the number of villeins on the estates of a ward
of the crown. That was a "waste of men" which impaired the
value of the lands, and the emancipation of his villeins infringed
the liberty of the lord. Just as one man's food is another man's
poison, one man's liberty was another's servitude. The liberties
which the barons hoped to secure at Runnymede were largely
composed of the services of their villeins. A liberty was in no
sense a common right or a popular conception. It has been defined as a portion of sovereign authority in the hands of a subject; and the popularity of liberty entirely depends upon the
extent of the portions and of their distribution. Medieval liberties were large, but their recipients were few. They were the
exceptions to the rule; it was because they were rare privileges
and not common rights that the framers of Magna Carta set so
much store upon liberties. When the house of commons began
to deal with the subject in Edward III's reign, it had a different
tale to tell; it begged the king, in 1348, to grant no more liberties

in the future. Every franchise or liberty was so much land and
so many people cut off from the common law, excluded from the
beneficent operation of king's writs and royal justice, and subjected to the arbitrary will of the owner of the liberty.

To redistribute and equalize liberty has been one of the principal functions of parliament; and the petition of 1348 is the
earliest indication of its grasp of the problem. But one of the
greatest obstacles to reform is commonly the reformers' frame of
mind; and the keenest opponents of other men's privileges are
often the stoutest defenders of their own. Parliamentary con-
centration on the task of reducing liberties was impeded by the
addiction of members to their own; and so long as constituencies
were evading parliamentary representation in order to lessen
their share in taxation and save the expense of members' wages,
the house of commons could not be a very efficient instrument
of reform. The local interest ever outweighed the common advantage during the middle ages; and parliaments, while they
gave vent to complaints, failed to enforce a remedy. The Good
parliament of 1376 was followed by a worthless successor, and
the commons by themselves were hardly able to compel the adoption of a single reform throughout the middle ages. It was not
they who checked Edward I, removed Edward II or Richard II,
or disposed of Henry VI or Richard III. Changes of government
were sometimes legalized in parliament, but they were made
outside, by unparliamentary methods and forces; and these same
forces which made and unmade kings were themselves the repositories of the "liberties" of which the commons complained. Indeed, the more they made free with the royal prerogative and
took liberties with the crown, the greater grew their own. "Get
you lordship," wrote one of the Paston correspondents in 1450,
"because there the whole Law and the Prophets are founded."
Lordship and liberty were much the same thing, and the over-
mighty subject grasped an ever-increasing share of sovereign
power. As late as Elizabeth's reign it was said that the men of
Northumberland would have no other prince than a Percy, and
in Yorkshire the sheriff had little power against the bailiffs and
stewards of the northern earls. The so-called constitutional experiment of the Lancastrians consisted in little more than giving
rein to the local liberties of the magnates, who in the Wars of the
Roses took the bit between their teeth.

The extent of the liberties claimed by these magnates is difficult to realize, but without some appreciation of it we cannot explain the Tudor autocracy or understand how that despotism coincided with a vast movement of national liberation. It was not merely that the over-mighty subject excluded royal writs from his franchise and defied the crown from his feudal castle. We now regard the armed forces of the nation as the armed forces of the crown, but then the crown controlled but a fraction of the military strength of England. Each magnate had his council of state, his council learned in the law, and his bands of armed retainers, with which he could do more or less as he liked. In a state trial of 1554 it was urged in defence of the Duke of Suffolk that there was nothing treasonable in a peer levying his forces and making proclamation that foreigners should quit the realm. Technically the contention was sound, but the picture of peers raising forces and making proclamations on their own account in the middle of the Tudor period indicates the largeness of their liberties. In Elizabeth's reign even members of her council considered it not incompatible with their loyalty to carry on diplomatic correspondence of their own with foreign powers and to invoke foreign assistance in their struggles with their colleagues. The law of treason, too, protected them as well as the crown; if an offence against the latter might be high treason, an offence against the former might be petty treason; and an act of Henry VII speaks of a man's master as being his sovereign. The idea of a single all-embracing national sovereign was still in the making, and lords still regarded themselves as princes enjoying sovereign liberties.

The destruction of these liberties was the great service rendered by the Tudors to the cause of English liberty. Parliament in the middle ages had failed to nationalize liberty; with the help of the crown that nationalization was achieved in the sixteenth century. Liberty was made more common by redistribution; the great liberties of the few were diminished, the meagre liberties of the mass increased; and dukes and serfs make a simultaneous disappearance from the England of William Shakespeare. The liberation was achieved, like most acts of emancipation, by despotic means. Even the act emancipating British slaves was passed in 1834 by a parliament in which the slaveholders were not represented and over which they had no con-

trol; emancipation was imposed by the north on the south of
the United States at the point of the bayonet; and it was an
autocrat of all the Russias who emancipated the Russian serf.
So it was the Tudor despots who emancipated England from its
medieval "liberties." Henry VII restrained the liberty of maintenance and deprived the nobles of their hosts of armed retainers; and by means of the Star chamber he checked their
liberty of packing, bribing, and intimidating juries. Henry VIII,
by an act of parliament, took many medieval "liberties" into
his hands; he improved upon the petition presented by the commons in 1348, and not only refrained from granting liberties, to
the hindrance of the common law and oppression of the common
people, but revoked the grants that had been made. The Tudor
prerogative courts, the councils of the North, of Wales, and so
forth, gathered into their hands the liberties of the marcher
lords, and reduced the realm to a common order.

Nor was it only lords whose liberties were restricted in the
interests of national freedom. The franchises of corporations
might be as fatal to general liberty as the privileges of peers.
Bacon described gilds as "fraternities in evil," Sir John Mason
thought corporations more hurtful to the realm than anything
else; and in 1682 the citizens of London were declared liable to
fine and imprisonment for "presuming to act as a corporation."
They, too, were possessed of portions of sovereign authority
which they used to the common detriment. London tried to im-
poverish other English cities by forbidding its merchants to frequent their markets, and England presented a welter of
conflicting and restricting municipal jurisdictions. The "freedom" which cities now confer on eminent politicians is a survival
from times and conditions in which every Englishman was a
foreigner outside his native town, with no liberties in any city
but his own. Nor did he possess much liberty even there.
Municipal independence was no guarantee of individual freedom; and in many a medieval city renowned for its fight against
despots the individual's liberty was confined by a minute and
meticulous regulation unknown to oriental tyranny. His every
act was regulated for him from the cradle to the grave. He could
not leave the parish in which he was born or the trade to which
he was bred, or carry on business except in accordance with
cast-iron rules. The necessities of self-defence in a limited space

compelled the closest formation, and individual liberty was a luxury which municipal independence could not afford. National strength and protection relieved the need for congestion. City walls and castle-keeps could disappear with civil war and feudal anarchy, and civic liberty could spread to the bounds of the sea behind the shield of a nation's navy. It was not mere chance that the dynasty which created England's fleet destroyed its civic independence and subjected municipal legislation to national control. By centralizing power the Tudors expanded English liberties and converted local privileges into a common national right.

They did it by means of parliament, and could not have done it without. For one thing, only the common feeling produced by the co-operation of local representatives at Westminster could have prepared the way for the requisite surrender of local prejudice and the merging of local in national liberty. For another, nothing less than an act of the crown in parliament could have constrained these local and personal liberties. It was sufficiently revolutionary that even an act of parliament should override a medieval liberty; for the notion of fundamental law was deeply ingrained in the medieval mind, and the possessors of liberties based their possession on a divine or natural law that was beyond and above the power of kings or parliaments. Magna Carta was long regarded as fundamental law, and repeated protests were made that all things done in contravention thereof, judicial or legislative, within or without parliament, should be regarded as null and void. The growth of positive law at the expense of divine and natural law, and of the idea that human will and mundane counsels could amend the foundations of society, is the beginning of the sovereignty of parliament. But without that overriding sovereignty to limit and abolish them, English medieval liberties would have petrified society on a mould of local and class particularism, and have produced that kind of ossification which stereotyped oriental communities and even reduced France to the necessity of bursting its social shell for the sake of expansion.

As it was, the crown in parliament secured a free hand through the tacit or actual surrender of the claim to indefeasible liberty on the part of individuals and associations. The attachment of the medieval mind to this autonomy was pronounced, and it has

been said that the indestructibility of the individual will was
the strongest characteristic of the middle ages. Even in the administration of justice the accused could refuse to submit to the
verdict of his country; he could "stand mute," *i. e.* decline to
plead. It is true that the one form of torture countenanced by
English law, the *peine forte et dure,* could be applied to over-
come this resistance; but if he died under its pressure, the court
had to go without its verdict. He died an innocent man and his
property could not be touched. When Henry VIII was attacking
the monasteries infinite pains were taken to secure "surrenders"
in preference, or at least as a preliminary, to parliamentary confiscation. In every sphere the particularist manifestation was
strong compared with the national, and parliaments only succeeded in overriding the individual because every Englishman
was "intended" to be present in parliament, and an act of
parliament was understood to be by representation the act of
every individual. Its sovereignty was the sum total of the will
of every member of the community. It monopolized power and
prepared the way for the Austinian dogma that law is the command of the state. Liberty therefore came to depend, not upon
an immutable divine or natural law, but upon the will of the
community as expressed in acts of parliament which could ex-
tend, restrict, or redistribute the various liberties possessed by
different classes.

The effect of this development of parliamentary power was to
make it possible to moderate the inequalities of medieval liberty;
and, while the overmighty subject suffered crushing blows in
Tudor times, the age was for the mass of English people one of
liberation. Liberty became a national matter rather than the
privilege of a class or a locality. Curious relics of local liberties
still remain; but for the most part these anomalies were, during
the sixteenth century, merged in common and equal rights
guaranteed by acts of parliament and enforced by royal or national law courts. It was the destruction of these barriers and
the fusion of classes that produced the intense national and
patriotic feeling of Elizabeth's reign. The trinity of estates fades
into the unity of the state.

25 FROM   *Émile Lousse*

Were There Really Only "Liberties"?

*In this paper Émile Lousse, Professor of History in the Uni-
versity of Louvain, takes a very different line from Pollard.
Pollard was concerned with the constitutional forms of liberty,
Lousse with its juridical nature. The two arguments present an
interesting contrast of English and continental scholarship. Professor Lousse's paper is reproduced in full.*

The freedom of man and animals is worth comparing. Some
animals range through the air, the waters or over the face of
the earth without let or hindrance, other than their natural
capacities or external danger. Others lead a more sedentary life
within a restricted area, great or small, as if encaged. Others
again enjoy relative security throughout their life; they cover
a wider radius than the sedentary animals and do so in complete
safety, but only because they are led and fed, and carry the
yoke or collar; remember the fable of the dog and the wolf.
Human freedom likewise is not cut to one single pattern. At its
widest, it is the liberty of Robinson Crusoe on his desert island
before he encountered Man Friday; but the story, let alone our
own experience and common sense, tells us that Robinson was
far from content with his lot, at least until he met his humble
companion. Within society, liberty in the legal sense is nothing
but a condition of voluntary commitment to the common good.
We may almost describe it as the permanent juridical condition
which arises from commitments entered upon to this end.

In the pages which follow, we intend to investigate what
liberty, conceived in this sense, meant in the juridical, social and
political structure of the Ancien Régime, and whether we are
forced to accept, as some have argued, that the Ancien Régime
differed from our own in that there was no liberty in the

SOURCE. É. Lousse, "N'y avait-il vraiment que 'des' Libertées." *Anciens
Pays et Assemblées d'Etats* (Louvain), vol. 9, 1955, pp. 69–76. Reprinted by
permission of Nauwelaerts Editions.

philosophical sense, but only liberties. We shall develop our theme in the light of many different sources which we have used for work already published or in the course of preparation: charters and formularies which refer to the services, liberties and status of both persons and corporate bodies, of communities, orders, provinces and countries. We shall proceed from the concrete to the abstract: from the particular guarantees protecting persons and property considered free (thereby excluding the non-free), to the overall condition of commitment to ends and means which lie outside the capacity of the individual and only become accessible to concerted effort.

Charters and formularies reveal with equal clarity that, in the Ancien Régime as now liberty is both civil and political and protects both persons and property. Every free man ought to be judged by his peers according to law; he ought to be consulted by his natural superiors on all decisions which particularly concern him, in matters legislative (statutes), fiscal (aids, taxes, impositions), social (customary services) and military (service under arms). "What touches all should be approved by all."[1] The free man must also be protected in the peaceful enjoyment of his goods. He cannot be deprived of them, without his prior consent, even by the indirect method of excessive taxation or offensive war abroad. His person and his property, including his home, are inviolable. The famous chapter 39 of the English Great Charter sums all this up for us.

We can reach the same conclusion by a kind of counter-proof if we start with the evidence about serfs: we mention serfs but we ought to remember too that there were also slaves, both enforced and voluntary. Now serfs are subject to compulsory taxation and services; when serfdom first appears, many of them are at the mercy of their lords. They enjoy no liberty of any kind, civil or political, in their persons or in their goods. They are subject to the lord's right to pursue and recapture them. Legally they are unable to leave the estate to which they are bound (like game in a park, or cattle in the field, or a horse at tether, or a dog in a kennel); they are incapable of establishing themselves elsewhere. They are equally incapable of achieving the same end by an indirect route; they may not contract a

1 See above p. 139 n. 1.

marriage without the consent of their lord, above all if they wish to marry someone of different status or from another manor. They are under a similar disability in managing their property. They cannot dispose of their servile tenements. They may only dispose of such goods as they may have accumulated, in submitting themselves to the lord's right to a portion of the bequest or sale, by servile payments which allow him to take his cut with the passage of each generation, if not even more frequently. By the simple fact of their birth they are forever bound to perform all kinds of services, in a condition which they have not chosen (unless they themselves agreed to submit to a contract of serfdom), and from which it is almost impossible for them to escape without the consent of the person who has the most direct interest in keeping them in his subjection. They are bound to perform service without return and without hope of emancipation by enfranchisement, either individual or collective.

This legal disability in the several forms which we have just discussed, is not limited to serfs and slaves. It reappears, usually as some kind of constraint or "dependence," in the status and condition of all those people, who even though of free birth, are placed for the common good in the power or protection of others: daughters of all ages whether married or not; sons not yet freed from parental control; illegitimate sons; adults under some kind of legal disability: lepers; foreign residents who are not incorporated legally in the life of the manor, lordship, town or country, but share its material resources; infidels, both pagan or relapsed who suffer similar legal disability in relation to the universal or dominant church; those condemned on political charges or at common law; prisoners of war; those penalised by total deprivation of civil rights, the most unworthy of all the unworthy; the religious, who are the sons or voluntary serfs of their monastic house, cut off from society in the cause of evangelical perfection. . . All these are incapable in law of disposing by themselves of their goods or persons, in marriage or otherwise. Indeed this whole range of disabilities includes serfdom, for serfdom is simply the incapacity to commit oneself to a freely chosen purpose. It is a legal disability which reinforces a social or natural disability. The serf is like a prisoner except that he has done no wrong. It is as though he has been declared insane. Society not only protects him from abuse by others but also guarantees itself against the possible excesses which may arise from his frailty.

Liberty does not consist in not being bound to another, but simply in not being bound despite oneself. It is not the same as independence or a total lack of ties. It is the legal capacity to contract such ties and to avoid bonds of any kind which are imposed on one by another without his consent. Individual liberty becomes all the greater as society, at any point in time, ceases to mistrust it and as the law in force at the time, with all its prejudices and faults as well as its clarity and justice, recognises each man's natural and legal capacities. The clearer it is seen by each individual the higher it stands as an objective in the organisation of the family, the city, the profession or the church. The legal capacity of the individual is made up of several distinct conditions: his position in the family, the state, in his order, his profession or religion. Under each heading each individual enjoys a particular capacity or disability. It is the addition of capacities and disabilities which determines his liberty. He is considered free, superior and privileged if his condition involves more capacities than disabilities, taking into account that his capacities serve the common interest. On the other hand he is considered a serf, inferior and unfree, if his condition is diminished by so many disabilities that he is considered incapable of contributing to the common good except under the power and direction of some person of greater capacity. Liberty results from the sum of these capacities: indeed it is that sum. The society of the Ancien Régime is not composed of equal persons, but of these two categories which liberty/capacity separate with a horizontal line. The free are able to dispose of themselves and their goods under the protection of the law; the unfree or incapable are placed by law in the power of a father, master or lord, who rules them and is publicly responsible for their good behaviour.

Which then is the predominant note? Which comes first liberty or legal capacity? The sources seem to state both lines of argument. According to some writers of the Ancien Régime society is composed on the one hand of those who enjoy legal superiority and competence and hence are counted free, and on the other of those who are in a state of legal disability and are relegated to a servile condition in the interests of public order.

To be under legal disability and unfree is almost one and the same thing, even though a theoretical distinction has to be made between those of free and servile stock. Other theorists of the period distinguish between free-born men, who are legally competent and exercise lawful power; and others who, according to the view of Georges de Ghewiet,[2] "are really free when compared with slaves but who, all in all, are under the power and authority"; villeins and serfs in fact.

There are many degrees both of freedom and servitude. But where is the line to be drawn between the highest degree of servitude and the lowest degree of freedom? Clearly minors of free birth, those distinguished by the word *liberi* and accorded non-patrimonial capacities in Roman times, are not treated in the same way as their father's slaves; they live in a different manner, even their dress is different, above all they have different expectations. But this does not alter the fact that their legal disability is similar to the slaves' and is based on the same social grounds; St. Paul himself developed the argument in one of his Epistles.[3] Wife, legitimate children and serfs are all passive members of each "house" or clan and then of each order, state or Church, and these in turn are nothing but stages in the association not of individuals, but of families, both natural and spiritual.

Family status exercises a decisive influence over the other elements in an individual's legal competence. Heads of families were the only really free men in ancient Rome; they had complete and active civic status, limited only by the requirements that they should participate in ancestor-worship and conduct a non-servile profession. Christianity altered this situation to some extent by making marriage, in undiminished form, available to slaves, thus marking the first stage in their emancipation. In the same way, during the middle ages and down to the end of the Ancien Régime the only real free men with full legal competence were the fathers of families, natural and spiritual, of non-servile status (this assumes of course that the fathers and

[2] Georges de Ghewiet, 1651–1745, Flemish jurist, author of *Institutions du droit Belgique*, 1736.

[3] Galatians, IV. 1. "Now I say, that the heir, as long as he is a child, differeth nothing from a servant, though he be lord of all."

their families were members of the dominant religion). The fathers of such families dominate the social structure: feudal, manorial, municipal and corporative. They are the only lords of their domain in the true sense. In a derivatory sense they are the only master-citizens or burgesses of their towns and the only masters fully qualified in their professions. In the same way the fathers of spiritual families, the vicar in his parish, the bishop in his diocese, superiors in their monastic house or orders, up to the Pope himself, govern and lead the ecclesiastical order, in each province as in the church universal.

Almost all these fathers of free families have taken the title of lord. They have authority; they claim 'their right and power', and therein lies their capacity to enter upon agreements with their neighbours. "Even a poor man is king in his own house"; among laymen there is no master of a household, however poor his lot, who does not exercise power which is at once marital, paternal and domainal. If he is unfree he will be under the power of another, but he is not essentially different in that from the son of the house, even of a great and noble family, who may marry and yet remain under the power of his father (at least in the countries governed by Roman Law). Among the nobility the head of a family enjoys power over his family and lands; he may also be a prince, a king or an emperor. Among the bourgoisie his power is not simply that of a head of a family or of a burgess or master of a profession: he may rise to high office in town or gild. The religious likewise may become superiors of their communities; clerks may become priests and vicars bishops; they may ascend every successive stage of status and authority up to the very highest.

These men of superior legal competence, who lawfully enjoy power and liberty, are also natural representatives. There are two kinds of representation: with or without mandate. In those relationships which we nowadays call private, the father represents the family, the simple household or the clan as the case may be, on the basis of a position which he owes to his marriage and his descent. He is responsible for representing the family or for arranging that he himself is represented in minor matters by giving a special mandate to one of those under his authority. In public life, the prince, lord or properly constituted head exercises lawful authority over the community and represents it without any special mandate. The governing body of a community may also command one of its members to represent it, under mandate, in such and such an affair, and to report to it thereon. Those who are under some legal disability, or are unfree or "inferior," must be represented by others, but the exercise of such representation is limited to those who enjoy full legal competence in the exercise of their powers and the enjoyment of their liberty.

The juridical idea of liberty has altered little throughout history: it is simply the faculty of disposing of oneself. As Voltaire said it is "property in one's person." In actual fact it is always restricted by the requirements of society and by philosophies derived from social utility. The Declaration of the Rights of Man, 26 August 1789, makes the point very clearly (article 4). "Liberty consists in the power to do anything which is not harmful to others. Hence the only limits to the natural rights of every man are those which guarantee the enjoyment of the same rights to other members of society. These limits can only be determined by law." Men probably thought in the same way before the French Revolution. For them, as for modern thinkers, civil liberty is that which allows a citizen to live in security under the protection of the law so long as he conforms to it. In all countries, liberty, authority and law are indispensible; they define public order and guarantee the common good. Changes arise from differences in region, period and the objectives of successive dominant groups. However, these do not modify the formal categories of liberty, authority and law, but rather the philosophy which defines the common good and, derived from that, the equally mutable philosophy which defines the natural rights of man, along with the guarantees with which those rights must be surrounded to ensure that they shall not be destroyed or impugned, but preserved and respected.

26   FROM   *Eugène Stevens*
What Is Liberty?

Eugène Stevens here develops some further points implicit in Lousse's argument. The whole of his paper is reproduced.

In one of his last stories in which the action is situated right in the heart of the Amazonian jungle, the American author, James Ramsey Ullman describes a little scene worth noting. One of the principal characters of the story is the representative of a corporation which has bought exclusive rights for the exploration and exploitation of oil in the region. He meets another prospector whom he tries to warn off by advancing the rights which his corporation has bought. He receives this reply: "Where do you think you are? In a court of law? Here your rights are worth about as much as snowballs in the sun." The hard cynicism of these words seems to express the law of the jungle. And yet they only seem to follow the words of Jean de la Fontaine, who was far from uncivilised: "the best right is always the right of the strongest." Can it be that justice, right, liberty are nothing more than utopian dreams? Are men simply predators? Are laws and codes nothing more than paper ramparts against violence and brutality? Philosophy has tried to answer these questions, with greater or less conviction. History may illuminate them. The idea of liberty lies at the heart of these problems. It is at the core of the many antagonisms which dominate human relationships: the power of governments versus the rights of those governed, force versus justice, the common good versus particular interest. This therefore will be the subject of this study.

It is some time since Professor Lousse, whom I must thank most sincerely, advised me to undertake a study in this field. He suggested that I should analyse as many public documents as

SOURCE. E. Stevens, "Quid est Libertas," *Anciens Pays et Assemblées d'Etats*, Louvain, vol. 22, 1961, pp. 219–225. Reprinted by permission of Nauwelaerts Editions.

possible, concerned with public law, of different countries and periods: Merovingian ordinances, Carolingian capitularies, feudal texts, communal charters, privileges of the Ancien Régime as well as modern constitutions. Comparison of such sources, widely scattered both chronologically and geographically, might lead me to a deeper analysis of liberty. This work is far from ended, but it is advanced enough to allow me to draw some preliminary conclusions which, through simple juxtaposition, may answer the question put in my title: What exactly is liberty? I intend to examine the successive changes which the concept of liberty has undergone in the course of west-European history, for it is there, where it has undergone least modification, that we shall most easily grasp its nature.

During my course in the Humanities my teachers carefully implanted the notion that the Ancien Régime formed a single whole, a clearly defined entity. They did not make clear to me why this was so or what the characteristics of this period were: a failure, to be honest which derives less from their obscurity than from my own lack of understanding. But they did emphasise that the French Revolution was a kind of barrier marking off two completely different epochs; like an iron curtain dividing, not the world, but two zones of time of which the one, before 1789, was devoted to serfdom and the absolute power of a small minority, and the other, after 1789, is the period of liberty, if not for all, then at least for the great majority.

Later, as my reading extended, I saw that they had given an accurate rendering of the views of learned historians, and in fact, in many of its aspects, the Ancien Régime is sharply distinguished from the modern world. Since then the idea of public good, which is the base of all social organisation, has developed profoundly. The notion of the sovereignty of the people is scarcely met before, and has become essential since, the Revolution. The unitary state is unquestionably a product of contemporary history. Religious toleration is also a relatively recent attitude. But Liberty, Liberty with a capital which is contrasted with poor, petty liberties, (in the plural), is Liberty exclusively attached to the nineteenth century? Let us see.

It is clear that Liberty, in so far as it existed before 1789, was the prerogative of a small but increasing number, at least in the public and political domain. Merovingian synods and Carolin-

gian councils comprised only magnates, prelates and high dig-
nitaries. Emperors and kings summoned to their feudal councils
only the most powerful among their barons. In time, however,
communes, universities, sometimes even country districts, sent
their representatives to provincial or general estates, and by the
seventeenth century some documents come to contain clear statements of the principle of the sovereignty of the people. (The
Agreement of the People of 15 January 1649, art. 2: "that the
Representative of the whole nation shall consist of four hundred
persons"; The Bill of Rights, of 23 October 1689, almost to a
day a hundred years before the Declaration of the Rights of
Man: "being now assembled in a full and free representative of
this nation.") However, these precursors of modern thinking may
easily be interpreted as abstractions which scarcely affected the
characteristic inequalities of the Ancien Régime. I would do this
all the more readily because I have insisted on these inequalities
in order to point out that they in no way affected the essential
nature of liberty. For there are no *a priori* reasons for maintaining that this limited liberty of the Ancien Régime was in any
way different from that of our own allegedly more liberal days.
It reflected a different social organisation, but the concept of
guarantees against the abuse of power was the same as our own.

In fact, the rights guaranteed by ancient charters or modern
constitutions are in essentials the same. To take a few typical
examples, everywhere and at all times they include liberty of
person, the guarantee of honest and equitable justice, the right
to control state expenditure, the inviolability of the home and
the right to exercise some control over the raising of troops. It
goes without saying that certain liberties, characteristic of particular periods, appear and disappear according to circumstances.
Freedom of worship was new-born in the eighteenth century.
Freedom of the press did not begin to make headway until 150
years after Théophraste Renaudot.[1] We still have to wait for the
complete freedom of radio or television or the use of nuclear en-
ergy. On the other hand, nobody, before the Great Discoveries,
thought of claiming the freedom of the seas, just as no-one today
would dream of rebelling in the cause of free right of pasture in

---

[1] Théophraste Renaudot: French physician (1586?–1653), Commissary General of the Poor under Cardinal Richelieu, he started the first French news-
paper, the *Gazette*, in 1631.

the common fields. Even though the most important liberties are immutable, liberty in its concrete applications may vary, yet without changing its essential quality.

What matters therefore is not the proportion of men who enjoy liberty—for this proportion depends on considerations external to the notion of liberty—nor is it the number of rights guaranteed—for this, which reveals how far liberty is enjoyed at any one time, depends on particular circumstances; what matters is the very existence of such rights, for once established, they give the subject guarantees against the possible abuse of governmental power. This unchanging essential quality of liberty acts as a thermostat or safety-valve between absolutism on the one hand and anarchy on the other. It is immutable in the sense that we can trace the notion long before as well as after the French Revolution. "It is in accordance with the law of God and human reason that lords who wish to be honoured and well served by their subjects will maintain their rights and customs for them, stable and intact, so long as they are not contrary to reason" (the charter of Countess Matilda of Portugal to the commune of Ghent, 1192, preamble). "Liberty consists in the power to do anything which is not harmful to others. Hence the only limits to the natural rights of every man are those which guarantee the enjoyment of the same rights to other members of society. These limits can only be determined by law" (Declaration of the Rights of Man, 26 August 1789, article 4). These two texts, separated by five centuries, express the same concern: that of ensuring normal working social relations by guaranteeing liberties within reasonable limits. If Matilda of Portugal speaks of the relationship between lord and man while the Constituent Assembly speaks of the relationship between man and society, this is because they draw on two different sets of politico-philosophical concepts; but this does not detract from their agreement on the nature of liberty; on the contrary.

Liberty, according to a truly attractive definition of Professor Lousse "does not consist in not being bound to another, but simply in not being bound despite oneself."[2] It ensures a reasonable balance between rights and duties, between public need and personal security, between the state and the individual, between

2 See above p. 162.

the common good and the particular interest. But liberty itself also requires guarantees, guarantees which, with the passage of time, have changed their form but not their function. Whether they take the form of a solemn oath, or the threat of anathema, or the right of rebellion, as in the Ancien Régime; or the oath to observe the law, or the principle of the sovereignty of the people, or the slow procedure of constitutional revision, as in our own time; the end remains the same: to provide the fundamental rights of the subject with the best possible defence against violation by superior authority.

Yet these guarantees prove insufficient. Despite the fact that ancient charters were conferred by the prince in the name of himself and his successors "in perpetuity and for ever," despite the fact that most of our present constitutions give the appearance of permanence, all these documents, without a single exception, have been violated, transgressed, repudiated, misinterpreted or abolished for a shorter or longer term. For proof of this we only need to look at the long list of texts of this kind. They are to be counted in thousands, perhaps in tens of thousands. Nothing is perhaps more revealing than the nomenclature by which they are described in the more important languages of western Europe; I have found·some seventy such terms and I have no doubt missed many. I have analysed several hundred charters of which most are confirmations. To the best of my knowledge, the Great Charter was confirmed on half a dozen occasions,[3] the charter of Kortenberg on two occasions,[4] the privileges acquired by Liège in 1208 by six different emperors, and the charter of the Normans by Louis XI in 1462.[5] And what do we learn from these numerous confirmations and renewals unless it is that the promises they contained were scarcely ever kept?

Moreover these promises have only rarely, perhaps never, been given completely freely. We must not be misled by such formulae as "we grant these privileges to the men of St. Omer because they

3 This is an underestimate; see above p. 59.

4 The reference is to the Charter of liberties granted at the abbey of Kortenberg, between Brussels and Louvain, by John, Duke of Brabant in 1312. It was confirmed in 1332 and 1372. See Suggestions for Further Reading, below pp. 189–90.

5 See above p. 131.

have behaved more honestly and faithfully towards me than have other Flemings" (charter of William Clito[6] to St. Omer, 14 April 1127, preamble) or "by the inspiration of God and for the safety of our soul" (Great Charter, 19 June 1215, preamble). In fact princes gave guarantees to their subjects only under compulsion; and they were eager to suppress them as soon as circumstances allowed, like John the Fearless[7] who confiscated the charters of Liège and the county of Looz after the battle of Othée (1408). Remember also the circumstances which forced John Lackland to seal the Great Charter. Guy de Dampierre,[8] on 15 May 1297, after prolonged tergivasations, at last confirmed the charters of Bruges which had been destroyed by a fire, but only because the leaders of the commune were siding with the king of France, who had also acknowledged their rights. Most of the charters of Brabant, beginning with the celebrated Joyeuse Entrée[9] (3 January, 1356) were granted by the dukes either because they urgently required financial help from their "faithful subjects" or because they wanted to avoid difficulties at an approaching succession. The charter of Tübingen of 1514 was purchased. The English Bill of Rights (1689) and the American Declaration of Independence sprang from an act of force. The numerous French constitutions were also born of rebellion, whilst the Russian constitutions, both of Lenin and Stalin, are the children of October 1917.

As with all human history, so the history of liberty is the history of the top- and under-dog. The Agreement of the People and the Bill of Rights represent a bid for liberty against two attempts, not very fruitful but real enough, at absolute power by the Stuart kings. Seen from this angle, the French Revolution of 1789 can be considered as the violent rebirth of a long suppressed liberty. For the order, peace and well-being of a community are a function of the equilibrium between the authority of rulers, concerned with the common good, and the good will and obedience of subjects, mindful of their private interests.

---

[6] William Clito (d. 1128) son of Duke Robert of Normandy and claimant to Normandy 1106–1127; claimant to Flanders 1127–1128.

[7] John the Fearless, duke of Burgundy, 1404–1419.

[8] Guy of Dampierre, court of Flanders, 1280–1305.

[9] *Joyeuse Entrée,* see above p. 140 n. 1.

Liberty—and with this definition I can conclude—is the expression of a relationship of these forces, the stake being the voluntary contribution of each individual to the common good.

Yet I would add two further points, if only to emphasise that this analysis of liberty is not so harsh as it may seem at first sight. Above the entrance to one of the wings of the building on the Quai des Orfèvres which shelters the administration of justice, one may read this motto: "the Sword is the Guardian of the Law." The rôle of the police could not be stated more clearly: namely to preserve order, if necessary by force. But we can parody it, still retaining its sense and perhaps at the same time giving it a deeper meaning: "the sword is the guardian of liberty." When authority has lost all goodwill and is replaced by force this is not the brute application of the law of the strongest; it is the final and only really effective guarantee of liberty, the guarantee of the equitable exercise of authority and the genuine pursuit of the common good. There are two elements in my definition of liberty—power and justice; the first is no more than a means of achieving the second. It is worth remembering that every attempt to suppress liberty has sooner or later been repaid by the re-establishment of that same liberty by force.

APPENDIX

Magna Carta, 1215
Translation

John, by the grace of God, King of England, Lord of Ireland, Duke of Normandy and Aquitaine, Count of Anjou, to the archbishops, bishops, abbots, earls, barons, justiciars, foresters, sheriffs, stewards, servants and all his officials and faithful subjects greeting. Know that we, from reverence for God and for the salvation of our soul and those of all our ancestors and heirs, for the honour of God and the exaltation of Holy Church and the reform of our realm, on the advice of our reverend fathers, Stephen, Archbishop of Canterbury, Primate of all England and Cardinal of the Holy Roman Church, Henry, Archbishop of Dublin, William of London, Peter of Winchester, Jocelin of Bath and Glastonbury, Hugh of Lincoln, Walter of Worcester, William of Coventry and Benedict of Rochester, bishops, Master Pandulf, subdeacon and member of the household of the lord pope, brother Aimeric, master of the knighthood of the Temple in England, and the noble men, William Marshal, Earl of Pembroke, William, Earl of Salisbury, William, Earl of Warenne, William, Earl of Arundel, Alan of Galloway, Constable of Scotland, Warin fitz Gerald, Peter fitz Herbert, Hubert de Burgh, seneschal of Poitou, Hugh de Neville, Matthew fitz Herbert, Thomas Basset, Alan Basset, Philip de Albini, Robert of Ropsley, John Marshal, John fitz Hugh and others, our faithful subjects:

SOURCE. J. C. Holt, *Magna Carta*, Cambridge University Press, 1965, pp. 317–337. Reprinted by permission of Cambridge University Press.

1. In the first place have granted to God and by this our present Charter have confirmed, for us and our heirs in perpetuity, that the English church shall be free, and shall have its rights undiminished and its liberties unimpaired; and we wish it thus observed, which is evident from the fact that of our own free will before the quarrel between us and our barons began, we conceded and confirmed by our charter, freedom of elections, which is thought to be of the greatest necessity and importance to the English church, and obtained confirmation of this from the lord pope Innocent III, which we shall observe and wish our heirs to observe in good faith in perpetuity. We have also granted to all the free men of our realm for ourselves and our heirs for ever, all the liberties written below, to have and hold, them and their heirs from us and our heirs.

2. If any of our earls or barons, or others holding of us in chief by knight service shall die, and at his death his heir be of full age and owe relief, he shall have his inheritance on payment of the ancient relief, namely the heir or heirs of an earl £100 for a whole earl's barony, the heir or heirs of a baron £100 for a whole barony, the heir or heirs of a knight 100s. at most for a whole knight's fee; and anyone who owes less shall give less according to the ancient usage of fiefs.

3. If, however, the heir of any such person has been under age and in wardship, when he comes of age he shall have his inheritance without relief or fine.

4. The guardian of the land of such an heir who is under age shall not take from the land more than the reasonable revenues, customary dues and services, and that without destruction and waste of men or goods. And if we entrust the wardship of the land of such a one to a sheriff, or to any other who is answerable to us for its revenues, and he destroys or wastes the land in his charge, we will take amends of him, and the land shall be entrusted to two lawful and prudent men of that fief who will be answerable to us for the revenues or to him to whom we have assigned them. And if we give or sell to anyone the wardship of any such land and he causes destruction or waste, he shall lose the wardship and it shall be transferred to two lawful and prudent men of the fief who shall be answerable to us as is aforesaid.

5. Moreover so long as the guardian has the wardship of the land, he shall maintain the houses, parks, preserves, fishponds, mills and the other things pertaining to the land from its revenues; and he shall restore to the heir when he comes of age all his land stocked with ploughs and wainage such as the agricultural season demands and the revenues of the estate can reasonably bear.

6. Heirs shall be given in marriage without disparagement, yet so that before marriage is contracted it shall be made known to the heir's next of kin.

7. After her husband's death, a widow shall have her marriage portion and her inheritance at once and without any hindrance; nor shall she pay anything for her dower, her marriage portion, or her inheritance which she and her husband held on the day of her husband's death; and she may stay in her husband's house for forty days after his death, within which period her dower shall be assigned to her.

8. No widow shall be compelled to marry so long as she wishes to live without a husband, provided that she gives security that she will not marry without our consent if she holds of us, or without the consent of the lord of whom she holds, if she holds of another.

9. Neither we nor our bailiffs will seize any land or rent in payment of a debt so long as the chattels of the debtor are sufficient to repay the debt; nor shall the sureties of the debtor be distrained so long as the debtor himself is capable of paying the debt; and if the principal debtor defaults in the payment of the debt, having nothing wherewith to pay it, the sureties shall be answerable for the debt; and, if they wish, they may have the lands and revenues of the debtor until they have received satisfaction for the debt they paid on his behalf, unless the principal debtor shows that he has discharged his obligations to the sureties.

10. If anyone who has borrowed from the Jews any amount, great or small, dies before the debt is repaid, it shall not carry interest as long as the heir is under age, of whomsoever he holds; and if that debt fall into our hands, we will take nothing except the principal sum specified in the bond.

11. And if a man dies owing a debt to the Jews, his wife may

have her dower and pay nothing of that debt; and if he leaves
children under age, their needs shall be met in a manner in
keeping with the holding of the deceased; and the debt shall be
paid out of the residue, saving the service due to the lords. Debts
owing to others than Jews shall be dealt with likewise.

12. No scutage or aid is to be levied in our realm except by
the common counsel of our realm, unless it is for the ransom of
our person, the knighting of our eldest son or the first marriage
of our eldest daughter; and for these only a reasonable aid is to
be levied. Aids from the city of London are to be treated likewise.

13. And the city of London is to have all its ancient liberties
and free customs both by land and water. Furthermore, we will
and grant that all other cities, boroughs, towns and ports shall
have all their liberties and free customs.

14. And to obtain the common counsel of the realm for the
assessment of an aid (except in the three cases aforesaid) or a
scutage, we will have archbishops, bishops, abbots, earls and
greater barons summoned individually by our letters; and we
shall also have summoned generally through our sheriffs and
bailiffs all those who hold of us in chief for a fixed date, with
at least forty days' notice, and at a fixed place; and in all letters
of summons we will state the reason for the summons. And when
the summons has thus been made, the business shall go forward
on the day arranged according to the counsel of those present,
even if not all those summoned have come.

15. Henceforth we will not grant anyone that he may take an
aid from his free men, except to ransom his person, to make his
eldest son a knight and to marry his eldest daughter once; and
for these purposes only a reasonable aid is to be levied.

16. No man shall be compelled to perform more service for
a knight's fee or for any other free tenement than is due there-
from.

17. Common pleas shall not follow our court but shall be
held in some fixed place.

18. Recognizances of novel disseisin, mort d'ancestor, and
darrein presentment shall not be held elsewhere than in the
court of the county in which they occur, and in this manner:
we, or if we are out of the realm our chief justiciar, shall send
two justices through each county four times a year who, with

four knights of each county chosen by the county, shall hold the said assizes in the county court on the day and in the place of meeting of the county court.

19. And if the said assizes cannot all be held on the day of the county court, so many knights and freeholders of those present in the county court on that day shall remain behind as will suffice to make judgements, according to the amount of business to be done.

20. A free man shall not be amerced for a trivial offence, except in accordance with the degree of the offence; and for a serious offence he shall be amerced according to its gravity, saving his livelihood; and a merchant likewise, saving his merchandise; in the same way a villein shall be amerced saving his wainage; if they fall into our mercy. And none of the aforesaid amercements shall be imposed except by the testimony of reputable men of the neighbourhood.

21. Earls and barons shall not be amerced except by their peers and only in accordance with the nature of the offence.

22. No clerk shall be amerced on his lay tenement except in the manner of the others aforesaid and without reference to the size of his ecclesiastical benefice.

23. No vill or man shall be forced to build bridges at river banks, except those who ought to do so by custom and law.

24. No sheriff, constable, coroner or other of our bailiffs may hold pleas of our Crown.

25. All shires, hundreds, wapentakes and ridings shall be at the ancient farm without any increment, except our demesne manors.

26. If anyone holding a lay fief of us dies and our sheriff or bailiff shows our letters patent of summons for a debt which the deceased owed us, it shall be lawful for the sheriff or our bailiff to attach and list the chattels of the deceased found in lay fee to the value of that debt, by the view of lawful men, so that nothing is removed until the evident debt is paid to us; and the residue shall be relinquished to the executors to carry out the will of the deceased. And if he owes us nothing, all the chattels shall be accounted as the deceased's saving their reasonable shares to his wife and children.

27. If any free man dies intestate, his chattels are to be distributed by his nearest relations and friends, under the super-

vision of the Church, saving to everyone the debts which the deceased owed him.

28. No constable or any other of our bailiffs shall take any mans' corn or other chattels unless he pays cash for them at once or can delay payment with the agreement of the seller.

29. No constable is to compel any knight to give money for castle-guard, if he is willing to perform that guard in his own person or by another reliable man, if for some good reason he is unable to do it himself; and if we take or send him on military service, he shall be excused the guard in proportion to the period of his service.

30. No sheriff or bailiff of ours or anyone else is to take horses or carts of any free man for carting without his agreement.

31. Neither we nor our bailiffs shall take other men's timber for castles or other work of ours, without the agreement of the owner.

32. We will not hold the lands of convicted felons for more than a year and a day, when the lands shall be returned to the lords of the fiefs.

33. Henceforth all fish-weirs shall be completely removed from the Thames and the Medway and throughout all England, except on the sea coast.

34. The writ called *praecipe* shall not, in future, be issued to anyone in respect of any holding whereby a free man may lose his court.

35. Let there be one measure of wine throughout our kingdom and one measure of ale and one measure of corn, namely the London quarter, and one width of cloth whether dyed, russet or halberjet, namely two ells within the selvedges. Let it be the same with weights as with measures.

36. Henceforth nothing shall be given or taken for the writ of inquisition of life or limb, but it shall be given freely and not refused.

37. If anyone holds of us by fee-farm, by socage or by burgage, and holds land of someone else by knight service, we will not, by virtue of that fee-farm, socage or burgage, have wardship of his heir or of land of his that belongs to the fief of another; nor will we have custody of that fee-farm or socage or burgage unless such fee-farm owes knight service. We will not have custody of the heir or land of anyone who holds of another by knight service,

by virtue of any petty sergeanty which he holds of us by the service of rendering to us knives or arrows or the like.

38. Henceforth no bailiff shall put anyone on trial by his own unsupported allegation, without bringing credible witnesses to the charge.

39. No free man shall be taken or imprisoned or disseised or outlawed or exiled or in any way ruined, nor will we go or send against him, except by the lawful judgement of his peers or by the law of the land.

40. To no one will we sell, to no one will we deny or delay right or justice.

41. All merchants are to be safe and secure in leaving and entering England, and in staying and travelling in England, both by land and by water, to buy and sell free from all maletotes by the ancient and rightful customs, except, in time of war, such as come from an enemy country. And if such are found in our land at the outbreak of war they shall be detained without damage to their persons or goods, until we or our chief justiciar know how the merchants of our land are treated in the enemy country; and if ours are safe there, the others shall be safe in our land.

42. Henceforth anyone, saving his allegiance due to us, may leave our realm and return safe and secure by land and water, save for a short period in time of war on account of the general interest of the realm and excepting those imprisoned and outlawed according to the law of the land, and natives of an enemy country, and merchants, who shall be treated as aforesaid.

43. If anyone dies who holds of some escheat such as the honours of Wallingford, Nottingham, Boulogne or Lancaster, or of other escheats which are in our hands and are baronies, his heir shall not give any relief or do any service to us other than what he would have done to the baron if that barony had been in a baron's hands; and we shall hold it in the same manner as the baron held it.

44. Henceforth men who live outside the forest shall not come before our justices of the forest upon a general summons, unless they are impleaded or are sureties for any person or persons who are attached for forest offences.

45. We will not make justices, constables, sheriffs or bailiffs who do not know the law of the land and mean to observe it well.

46. All barons who have founded abbeys of which they have charters of the kings of England, or ancient tenure, shall have custody thereof during vacancies, as they ought to have.

47. All forests which have been afforested in our time shall be disafforested at once; and river banks which we have enclosed in our time shall be treated similarly.

48. All evil customs of forests and warrens, foresters and war-reners, sheriffs and their servants, river banks and their wardens are to be investigated at once in every county by twelve sworn knights of the same county who are to be chosen by worthy men of the county, and within forty days of the inquiry they are to be abolished by them beyond recall, provided that we, or our justiciar, if we are not in England, first know of it.

49. We will restore at once all hostages and charters delivered to us by Englishmen as securities for peace or faithful service.

50. We will dismiss completely from their offices the relations of Gerard d'Athée that henceforth they shall have no office in England, Engelard de Cigogné, Peter and Guy and Andrew de Chanceux, Guy de Cigogné, Geoffrey de Martigny with his brothers, Philip Marc with his brothers and his nephew, Geoffrey, and all their followers.

51. Immediately after concluding peace, we will remove from the kingdom all alien knights, crossbowmen, sergeants and mercenary soldiers who have come with horses and arms to the hurt of the realm.

52. If anyone has been disseised or deprived by us without lawful judgement of his peers of lands, castles, liberties or his rights we will restore them to him at once; and if any disagreement arises on this, then let it be settled by the judgement of the Twenty-Five barons referred to below in the security clause. But for all those things of which anyone was disseised or deprived without lawful judgement of his peers by King Henry our father, or by King Richard our brother, which we hold in our hand or which are held by others under our warranty, we shall have respite for the usual crusader's term; excepting those cases in which a plea was begun or inquest made on our order before we took the cross; when, however, we return from our pilgrimage, or if perhaps we do not undertake it, we will at once do full justice in these matters.

53. We shall have the same respite, and in the same manner,

in doing justice on disafforesting or retaining those forests which King Henry our father or Richard our brother afforested, and concerning custody of lands which are of the fee of another, the which wardships we have had hitherto by virtue of a fee held of us by knight's service, and concerning abbeys founded on fees other than our own, in which the lord of the fee claims to have a right. And as soon as we return, or if we do not undertake our pilgrimage, we will at once do full justice to complainants in these matters.

54. No one shall be taken or imprisoned upon the appeal of a woman for the death of anyone except her husband.

55. All fines which were made with us unjustly and contrary to the law of the land, and all amercements imposed unjustly and contrary to the law of the land, shall be completely remitted or else they shall be settled by the judgement of the Twenty-Five barons mentioned below in the security clause, or by the judgement of the majority of the same, along with the aforesaid Stephen, Archbishop of Canterbury, if he can be present, and others whom he wishes to summon with him for this purpose. And if he cannot be present the business shall nevertheless proceed without him, provided that if any one or more of the aforesaid Twenty-Five barons are in such a suit they shall stand down in this particular judgement, and shall be replaced by others chosen and sworn in by the rest of the same Twenty-Five, for this case only.

56. If we have disseised or deprived Welshmen of lands, liberties or other things without lawful judgement of their peers, in England or in Wales, they are to be returned to them at once; and if a dispute arises over this it shall be settled in the March by judgement of their peers; for tenements in England according to the law of England, for tenements in Wales according to the law of Wales, for tenements in the March according to the law of the March. The Welsh are to do the same to us and ours.

57. For all those things, however, of which any Welshman has been disseised or deprived without lawful judgement of his peers by King Henry our father, or King Richard our brother, which we have in our possession or which others hold under our legal warranty, we shall have respite for the usual crusader's term; excepting those cases in which a plea was begun or inquest made on our order before we took the cross. However, when we return,

or if perhaps we do not go on our pilgrimage, we will at once give them full justice in accordance with the laws of the Welsh and the aforesaid regions.

58. We will restore at once the son of Llywelyn and all the hostages from Wales and the charters delivered to us as security for peace.

59. We will treat Alexander, King of the Scots, concerning the return of his sisters and hostages and his liberties and rights in the same manner in which we will act towards our other barons of England, unless it ought to be otherwise because of the charters which we have from William his father, formerly King of the Scots; and this shall be determined by the judgement of his peers in our court.

60. All these aforesaid customs and liberties which we have granted to be held in our realm as far as it pertains to us towards our men, shall be observed by all men of our realm, both clerk and lay, as far as it pertains to them, towards their own men.

61. Since, moreover, we have granted all the aforesaid things for God, for the reform of our realm and the better settling of the quarrel which has arisen between us and our barons, and since we wish these things to be enjoyed fully and undisturbed, we give and grant them the following security: namely, that the barons shall choose any twenty-five barons of the realm they wish, who with all their might are to observe, maintain and cause to be observed the peace and liberties which we have granted and confirmed to them by this our present charter; so that if we or our justiciar or our bailiffs or any of our servants offend against anyone in any way, or transgress any of the articles of peace or security, and the offence is indicated to four of the aforesaid twenty-five barons, those four barons shall come to us or our justiciar, if we are out of the kingdom, and shall bring it to our notice and ask that we will have it redressed without delay. And if we, or our justiciar, should we be out of the kingdom, do not redress the offence within forty days from the time when it was brought to the notice of us or our justiciar, should we be out of the kingdom, the aforesaid four barons shall refer the case to the rest of the twenty-five barons and those twenty-five barons with the commune of all the land shall distrain and distress us in every way they can, namely by seizing castles, lands and possessions, and in such other ways as they can, saving our person and

those of our queen and of our children until, in their judgement, amends have been made; and when it has been redressed
they are to obey us as they did before. And anyone in the land
who wishes may take an oath to obey the orders of the said
twenty-five barons in the execution of all the aforesaid matters,
and to join with them in distressing us to the best of his ability,
and we publicly and freely permit anyone who wishes to take
the oath, and we will never forbid anyone to take it. Moreover
we shall compel and order all those in the land who of themselves and of their own free will are unwilling to take an oath
to the twenty-five barons to distrain and distress us with them,
to take the oath as aforesaid. And if any of the twenty-five barons
dies or leaves the country or is otherwise prevented from dis-
charging these aforesaid duties, the rest of the aforesaid barons
shall on their own decision choose another in his place, who
shall take the oath in the same way as the others. In all matters
the execution of which is committed to those twenty-five barons,
if it should happen that the twenty-five are present and disagree
among themselves on anything, or if any of them who has been
summoned will not or cannot come, whatever the majority of
those present shall provide or order is to be taken as fixed and
settled as if the whole twenty-five had agreed to it; and the aforesaid twenty-five are to swear that they will faithfully observe all
the aforesaid and will do all they can to secure its observance.
And we will procure nothing from anyone, either personally or
through another, by which any of these concessions and liberties
shall be revoked or diminished; and if any such thing is pro-
cured, it shall be null and void, and we will never use it either
ourselves or through another.

62. And we have completely remitted and pardoned to all
any ill will, grudge and rancour that have arisen between us and
our subjects, clerk and lay, from the time of the quarrel. Moreover we have fully forgiven and completely condoned to all,
clerk and lay, as far as pertains to us, all offences occasioned by
the said quarrel from Easter in the sixteenth year of our reign to
the conclusion of peace. And moreover we have caused letters
patent of the Lord Stephen, Archbishop of Canterbury, the Lord
Henry, Archbishop of Dublin, the aforesaid bishops and Master
Pandulf to be made for them on this security and the aforesaid
concessions.

63. Wherefore we wish and firmly command that the English Church shall be free, and the men in our realm shall have and hold all the aforesaid liberties, rights and concessions well and peacefully, freely and quietly, fully and completely for them and their heirs of us and our heirs in all things and places for ever, as is aforesaid. Moreover an oath has been sworn, both on our part and on the part of the barons, that all these things aforesaid shall be observed in good faith and without evil intent. Witness the above-mentioned and many others. Given under our hand in the meadow which is called Runnymede between Windsor and Staines on the fifteenth day of June in the seventeenth year of our reign.

SUGGESTIONS FOR FURTHER READING

GENERAL WORKS ON MAGNA CARTA

The modern study of Magna Carta begins with William Blackstone, *The Great Charter and the Charter of the Forest,* Oxford, 1759, reprinted in his *Law Tracts* vol. 2, 1762. The next great landmark is W. S. McKechnie, *Magna Carta,* first edition, Glasgow, 1905, and a considerably amended second edition, Glasgow, 1914. This book is out of date as regards its political commentary but is still the only work to attempt a comprehensive clause-by-clause commentary; it is still valuable. The 750th anniversary in 1965 led to an outburst of work. J. C. Holt, *Magna Carta,* Cambridge, 1965, is an extended examination of the charter and its background, with some comment on its later history. The *Magna Carta Essays,* published by the University Press of Virginia under the general direction of Professor A. E. Dick Howard, cover a range of topics both legal and historical. *The Great Charter, four essays on Magna Carta and the History of Our Liberty,* ed. Erwin N. Griswold, New York 1965, is a short volume made up of essays by Professor S. E. Thorne, Professor W. H. Dunham, Jr., Professor P. B. Kurland, and Sir Ivor Jennings. There is also an excellent short essay by Professor V. H. Galbraith, "Runnymede Revisited," in *Proceedings of the American Philosophical Society,* CX (1966), 307–317. Part of Professor Helen M. Cam's essay *Magna Carta—Event or Document?* has been printed in this volume (no. 15). See also J. E. A. Jolliffe, "Magna Carta," *Schweizer Beiträge zur Allgemeinen Geschichte,* Vol. 10, 1952, pp. 88–103. *Magna Carta Commemoration Essays,* ed. H. E. Malden, The Royal Historical Society, London, 1917 still remains useful. There are essays on Magna Carta in G. B. Adams, *The Origins of the English Constitution,* first edition, New

Haven, 1912, second edition, New Haven, 1920, C. H. McIlwain, *Constitutionalism and the Changing World*, Cambridge, 1939, and V. H. Galbraith, *Studies in the Public Records*, London, 1948. Jenks's view of the charter is reasserted in C. Petit-Dutaillis, *Studies and Notes supplementary to Stubbs's · Constitutional History*, vol. 1, trans. W. E. Rhodes, Manchester University Press, 1908.

TEXTS

Texts of the different versions of the charter and other relevant documents are included in the works by Blackstone, McKechnie and Holt given above. C. Bémont, *Chartes des Libertés Anglaises*, Paris, 1892, is also a reliable collection, as of course is Stubbs's *Select Charters*, best used in the ninth edition, ed. H. W. C. Davis, Oxford, 1921. Also useful are J. C. Dickinson, *The Great Charter, a translation with an introduction and notes*, Historical Association, London, 1955, G. R. C. Davis, *Magna Carta*, British Museum, London, 1963, and A. E. Dick Howard, *Magna Carta, Text and Commentary*, University Press of Virginia, Charlottesville, 1964.

SPECIAL ASPECTS

The documents themselves, their drafting and publication, are the main objects of study in the following: R. L. Poole, "The publication of Great Charters by the English Kings," *English Historical Review*, XXVIII (1913), 444–453, A. B. White, "The name Magna Carta," *English Historical Review*, XXX (1915), 472–475, XXXII (1917), 554–555, J. C. Fox, "The Originals of the Great Charter," *English Historical Review*, XXXIX (1924), 321–336, G. C. Crump, "The execution of the Great Charter," *History*, XIII (1928), 247–253, A. J. Collins, "The Documents of the Great Charter," *Proceedings of the British Academy*, XXXIV (1948), 233–279, C. R. Cheney, "The Eve of Magna Carta," *Bulletin of the John Rylands Library*, XXXVIII (1956), 311–341, J. C. Holt, "The Making of Magna Carta," *English Historical Review*, LXXII (1957), 401–422, C. R. Cheney, "The Twenty-Five Barons of Magna Carta," *Bulletin of the John Rylands Library*, L (1968), 280–307, and V. H. Galbraith, "A Draft of Magna Carta (1215)," *Proceedings of the British Academy*, LIII (1967), 345–360.

On the negotiations of 1215 the papers by Cheney, Galbraith and Holt listed above are important. See also F. M. Powicke, "The Bull 'Miramur plurimum' and a Letter to Archbishop Stephen Langton," *English Historical Review,* XLIV (1929), 86–93, and H. G. Richardson, "The Morrow of the Great Charter," *Bulletin of the John Rylands Library,* XXVIII (1944), 422–443, XXIX (1945), 184–200. For the negotiations of the opposing parties with the Papal Curia and the text and translation of many relevant documents see *Selected Letters of Pope Innocent III concerning England,* ed. C. R. Cheney and W. H. Semple, Nelsons Medieval Texts, London, 1963; the annotations to these letters are particularly useful and important. Further texts are supplied in *The Letters of Pope Innocent III (1198–1216) concerning England and Wales,* ed. C. R. Cheney and Mary G. Cheney, Oxford, 1967. See also G. B. Adams, "Innocent III and the Charter," in *Magna Carta Commemoration Essays,* London, 1917, 26–45. For the extensive periodical literature on a precursor of Magna Carta, the so-called "unknown" charter see J. C. Holt, *Magna Carta,* Cambridge, 1965, appendix 2.

GENERAL WORKS ON ANGEVIN GOVERNMENT AND THE REIGN OF KING JOHN

The most up-to-date biography of King John is W. L. Warren, King John, London, 1961; this is best read in the paperback edition, Penguin Books, 1966. Kate Norgate, *John Lackland,* London, 1902, is still rewarding reading. J. C. Holt, *King John,* Historical Association, London, 1963, is particularly concerned with the assessment of John's character and abilities by contemporaries and later historians. V. H. Galbraith, *Roger Wendover and Matthew Paris,* Glasgow, 1944, is an important study of the monastic chronicler's tradition of King John. The most comprehensive survey of the reign is S. Painter, *The Reign of King John,* Johns Hopkins Press, Baltimore, 1949. The origins of the rebellion of 1215 are examined in J. C. Holt, *The Northerners, a study in the reign of King John,* Oxford, 1961, and *The Making of Magna Carta,* University Press of Virginia, Charlottesville, 1965.

For general background students should first consult Doris M. Stenton, *English Society in the Early Middle Ages,* third edition, Pelican Books London, 1962, and A. L. Poole, *From Domesday*

Book to Magna Carta, second edition, Oxford, 1955. J. E. A. Jolliffe, *Angevin Kingship,* London, 1955, is an important and highly individual book marred by inaccuracy. For questions of feudal prerogatives and obligations A. L. Poole, *Obligations of Society in the Twelfth and Thirteenth Centuries,* Oxford, 1946, and S. Painter, *Studies in the History of the English Feudal Barony,* Johns Hopkins Press, Baltimore, 1943, should be consulted. On legal development see Doris M. Stenton, "King John and the Courts of Justice," *Proceedings of the British Academy,* XLIV (1958) 103–128, reprinted in her *English Justice between the Norman Conquest and the Great Charter,* The American Philosophical Society, Philadelphia, 1965. The definitive book on the loss of Normandy is F. M. Powicke, *The Loss of Normandy,* Manchester, 1913, second edition, 1961. F. M. Powicke, *Stephen Langton,* Oxford, 1928, and S. Painter, *William Marshal,* Johns Hopkins Press, Baltimore, 1933, are important biographical studies of two central figures.

Powicke's biography of Langton is the central work on Magna Carta and the Church. Students should consult the items listed above on the negotiations with the Papal Curia; also C. R. Cheney, "The Church and Magna Carta," *Theology,* LXVIII (1965), 266–272, and J. W. Gray, "The Church and Magna Carta in the century after Runnymede," *Historical Studies* (Papers read before the Irish Conference of Historians), VI (1968), 23–38. For the earlier relationships between King John and the Church see C. R. Cheney, "The alleged deposition of King John," *Studies in Medieval History presented to F. M. Powicke,* Oxford, 1948, 100–116; "King John and the Papal Interdict," *Bulletin of the John Rylands Library,* XXXIII (1956), 295–317; "King John's reaction to the Interdict on England," *Transactions of the Royal Historical Society,* fourth series, XXXI (1949), 129–150.

THE LATER HISTORY OF MAGNA CARTA

This is now covered in a number of comprehensive works which are themselves based on a voluminous periodical and monograph literature. The most important are, for the thirteenth century, Faith Thompson, *The First Century of Magna Carta: Why it persisted as a document,* Research Publications of the University of Minnesota, Minneapolis, 1925; Doris M. Stenton, *After Runnymede, Magna Carta in the Middle Ages,* University Press of Virginia, Charlottesville, 1965; for the period between the fourteenth century and the early seventeenth century, Faith Thompson, *Magna Carta, its role in the making of the English Constitution, 1300–1629,* University of Minnesota Press, Minneapolis, 1948. Among the many books which discuss the importance of Magna Carta in the sixteenth and seventeenth centuries are H. Butterfield, *The Englishman and his History,* Cambridge, 1944; J. G. A. Pocock, *The Ancient Constitution and the Feudal Law,* Cambridge, 1957; J. W. Gough, *Fundamental Law in English Constitutional History,* Oxford, 1961; Maurice Ashley, *Magna Carta in the Seventeenth Century,* University Press of Virginia, Charlottesville, 1965; and H. Butterfield, *Magna Carta in the Historiography of the Sixteenth and Seventeenth Centuries,* Stenton Lecture, University of Reading, 1969.

The later history of the charter to the present day is covered in two recent volumes: for America, A. F. Dick Howard, *The Road from Runnymede, Magna Carta and Constitutionalism in America,* University Press of Virginia, Charlottesville, 1968 and for England, Anne Pallister, *Magna Carta: the Heritage of Liberty,* Oxford, 1971.

Among the Magna Carta Essays published by the University Press of Virginia there are Gottfried Dietze, *Magna Carta and Property* (1965); Yale Kamisar, Fred E. Inbau, Thurman Arnold, *Criminal Justice in our Time* (1965); A. L. Goodhardt, *Law of the Land* (1966); and Daniel John Meador, *Habeas Corpus and Magna Carta* (1966), all of which are concerned with the later development of the charter.

COMPARATIVE STUDIES

This area is the least well served of all Magna Carta studies. W. Näf, *Herrschaftsverträge des Spätmittelalters,* Quellen zur neueren Geschichte, Bern 1951, brings together texts and German translations of the Golden Bull of Hungary, the Aragonese privileges of 1283 and 1287, the Joyeuse Entrée of Brabant, 1356, and later German privileges. R. von Keller, *Freiheitsgarantien für Person und Eigentum im Mittelalter,* Heidelberg, 1933, is still valuable. There are, of course, many works on the structure of medieval states in which charters of liberties are discussed.

É. Lousse, *La Société d'Ancien Régime,* Louvain, 1943, and F. Kern, *Kingship and Law in the Middle Ages,* trans. S. B. Chrimes, Oxford, 1956, a translation of *Gottesgnadentum und Widerstandsrecht im fruheren Mittelalter,* Leipzig, 1914, and H. Mitteis, *Der Staat des hohen Mittelalters,* Weimar, fifth edition 1962, are particularly useful. For the canonical background to secular notions, see Walter Ullmann, *Principles of Government and Politics in the Middle Ages,* London, 1961.

The best account of the French charters is A. Artonne, *Le mouvement de 1314 et les chartes provinciales de 1315,* Paris, 1912. E. Hantos, *The Magna Carta of the English and the Hungarian Constitution,* London, 1904, is out of date and unsatisfactory. Students should consult, Ch. d'Eszlary, "L'influence des Assises de Jerusalem sur la Bulle d'Or hongroise," *Le Moyen Age,* 1954, 335–378. Jos. van der Straeten, *Het Charter en de Raad van Kortenberg,* Studies presented to the International Commission for the history of Representative and Parliamentary Institutions, XII, XIII, 1952, is an important contribution to the history of liberties in the Low Countries; vol. XIII contains a summary of the work in French. For the Joyeuse Entrée of 1356 see the scholarly edition by R. van Bragt, *De Blijde Inkomst van de Hertogen van Brabant, Johanna en Wenceslas,* Standen en Landen ("Anciens Pays et Assemblées d'états"), 1956 and E. Lousse, "La Joyeuse Entrée brabanconne du 3 janvier 1356," *Schweizer Beiträge zur allgemeinen Geschichte,* X, 1952, 139–162. For the earlier German liberties see G. Barraclough, *The Origins of Modern Germany,* Oxford, 1947, and for the later, F. L. Carsten, *Princes and Parliaments in Germany from the fifteenth to the eighteenth century,* Oxford, 1959. On Spain see Luis de Valdeavellano, *Historia de las Instituciones Españolas,* Madrid, 1968, and the bibliography therein. For a scholarly study of legendary offshoots of the Aragonese liberties see R. A. Giesey, *If Not, Not,* Princeton, 1968.

BIBLIOGRAPHY

J. C. Holt, *Magna Carta,* Cambridge, 1965, contains a full bibliography up to that date. Faith Thompson, *Magna Carta, its role in the making of the English constitution 1300–1629,* Minneapolis, 1948, and Anne Pallister, *Magna Carta: the Heritage of Liberty,* Oxford, 1971, contain bibliographies on the later history of the charter.

GLOSSARY

Aid. Tax assessed on free tenants, except in certain specified cases (see Magna Carta cap. 12) subject to their consent.

Amercement. Usually a monetary penalty, the payer buying himself out of the mercy of the king.

Appeal. Criminal charge brought by a private person.

Arrière-ban. General levy of able-bodied freemen for defence of the land in an emergency.

Burgage. Tenure by which property, usually land or houses, is held in a borough.

Common Pleas. Civil actions between party and party, usually initiated by a writ.

Coram Rege. "Before" or "in the presence of" the king; hence court or justices *coram rege* accompany the king's itinerary, as opposed to the bench which sits at a fixed place, usually Westminster.

Darrein Presentment. Assize and writ of: procedure for empanelling a jury to determine patronage of an ecclesiastical benefice by declaring which patron had presented to the living on the last occasion.

Disparagement. Marriage to a social inferior, very frequently a foreigner.

Disseisin. Deprivation of estate, dispossession.

Escheat. Land which has reverted to a feudal lord, especially the Crown, on lack of a lawful heir or claimant, or through default by the tenant.

Eyre. Judicial circuit: a general eyre is not one held generally throughout the realm but one which has general powers defined by the articles of the eyre, that is the judges' commission.

Fee-Farm. Freehold held by payment of an annual rent.

Fine. Agreement, especially between litigants, or where a subject "fines" to obtain privileges from the King; whence the *Rolls of Fines and Offerings* which record such transactions.

Franchise. Interchangeable with a right or a liberty; frequently a right which involves private possession of some aspect of public authority, usually enjoyed by grant of that authority.

Honour. A large feudal complex or barony; hence honorial court; used more generally in continental sources, sometimes interchangeably with barony, sometimes with reference to high royal office, not infrequently in both these senses together.

Hundred. Subdivision of a shire.

Inspeximus. Charter in which an earlier charter is inspected, quoted verbatim, and confirmed.

Mesne. Intermediate.

Mesne Lord or Tenant. Intermediate lord or tenant between a tenant who holds in demesne and a feudal superior.

Mesne Process. Intermediate procedures between initiation and conclusion of legal action, civil or criminal, for example, seizure of land, stock or chattels, arrest or bail.

Mort d'Ancestor. Assize or writ of, procedure for empanelling a jury to determine succession to freehold.

Mortmain. Ecclesiastical property granted to the church as free alms from which no secular service is due.

Novel Disseisin. Assize or writ of, procedure for empanelling a jury to determine case of recent dispossession of freehold.

Praecipe. Literally the imperative "instruct", "order": writ *praecipe* [*quod reddat*]: writ directing restoration of estate under sanction of summons to royal court.

Relief. Money paid by an heir for admission to freehold inheritance.

Riding. Subdivision of a shire.

Scutage. Usually money paid as commutation of knight service, assessed at a specific sum per knight's fee or shield (*scutum*): more generally any tax assessed in this way.

Socage. Tenure of freehold by fixed services, excluding knight-service, sergeanty and free alms, usually by payment of rent.

Tallage. Tax levied by a lord on unfree tenants, without consent, whence *taille.*

Tourn. Special half-yearly visitation by sheriff of courts of hundred or wapentake.

Wainage. Yield or profit of cultivated land.

Wapentake. Subdivision of a shire, characteristic of the Danish areas of England.